SOV E II R EIGN

A CELEBRATION OF FORTY YEARS OF SERVICE

HER MAJESTY THE QUEEN'S
40TH ANNIVERSARY

SOV E II R EIGN

A CELEBRATION OF FORTY YEARS OF SERVICE

INTRODUCED BY

JOHN JULIUS NORWICH

HER MAJESTY THE QUEEN'S
40TH ANNIVERSARY

C&B

COLLINS & BROWN

Frontispiece
The Machin Portrait.
This has been in use
on stamps and coins
since the 1960s.

First published in Great Britain in 1992
by Collins & Brown Limited
Mercury House
195 Knightsbridge
London SW7 1RE

British Library Cataloguing-in-Publication Data
A catalogue record for this book
is available from the British Library.
ISBN 1 85585 116 4

Edited and designed by Collins & Brown Limited
Art Director **Roger Bristow**
Designed by **Steven Wooster**

Filmset by Spectrum, London
Reproduction by Daylight, Singapore
Printed and bound in Great Britain by BPCC Hazell Books, Paulton

Page 8
The Queen with her
first grandchild, Peter
Philips, on her 52nd
birthday, photographed
by Snowdon.

CONTENTS

SOV E II R EIGN

T HE ROYAL COLLEGE OF ART is very greatly honoured to have been commissioned by The Royal Anniversary Trust to design and construct the SOVEREIGN exhibition, a celebration of forty years of service by Her Majesty Queen Elizabeth II.

I would like to thank Lord Norwich very much indeed for agreeing to become Curator and Christopher Frayling the College Curator and for their inspiration and hard work. It has been a particular pleasure working with Elizabeth Esteve-Coll and her staff at the Victoria and Albert Museum and I am deeply grateful to her and them for their help and cooperation.

Finally, I wish to record my appreciation of the work and individual contributions made by every member of the Executive Committee and of the staff and students of the College and others who have helped to put the SOVEREIGN exhibition together, not forgetting Ruth Anders, who as Project Director has held it all together in a magnificent manner.

JOCELYN STEVENS
RECTOR
ROYAL COLLEGE OF ART

$\mathcal{P}$REFACES

THE ROYAL ANNIVERSARY TRUST was established in 1990 to bring about a suitable programme of events to celebrate the fortieth anniversary of the Queen's accession to the throne in 1992. This programme of celebration enables people to express their gratitude to the Queen for her outstanding service to the nation over the forty years.

One of the Trust's most important events is the SOVEREIGN exhibition. It has been designed by The Royal College of Art (Design) Limited and is sponsored by The Daily Telegraph, Pearson and Reed International. We are greatly indebted to them all, and to the Victoria and Albert Museum, for helping to produce such a spectacular display. It is intended to provide the visitor with a unique view of the wide range of the Queen's duties and interests as our Head of State.

We hope you will enjoy it.

ROBIN GILL

HER MAJESTY THE QUEEN'S
40TH ANNIVERSARY

GEORGE YOUNGER

WE ARE DELIGHTED TO BE celebrating the fortieth year of the reign of Her Majesty Queen Elizabeth II, and, as sponsors of the SOVEREIGN exhibition, to be helping to mark this anniversary of Her Majesty's accession. As publishers of some of Britain's most widely read newspapers, magazines and books, we have for many years reported on the major developments and people of the day. We are particularly pleased, therefore, to support this superb exhibition, which so fully reflects the extent of Her Majesty's activities and achievements.

CONRAD BLACK
CHAIRMAN

MICHAEL BLAKENHAM
CHAIRMAN

PETER DAVIES
CHAIRMAN

The Daily Telegraph

 ·PEARSON·

 REED INTERNATIONAL

$\mathcal{I}$NTRODUCTION

W HEN THE ROYAL ANNIVERSARY TRUST decided to commission the SOVEREIGN exhibition, they knew that they would be breaking entirely new ground. No previous exhibition in the history of these islands has attempted to explain the nature of our British monarchy; nor has one ever been focused on a single reigning monarch. And this, it must be admitted, is hardly surprising: in earlier days any such exhibition would probably been seen a *Lèse-majesté*, and would anyway have been virtually impossible without modern technology.

But, as SOVEREIGN will make abundantly clear, much else has also occurred in the four decades that have so far marked the reign of Queen Elizabeth II. Not only has our exhibition technology advanced by leaps and bounds; there have also been changes, almost as dramatic, in our conception of the monarchy itself. Although it remains as popular as ever it was, the vastly increased powers of the press, radio and, above all, television have brought it far closer to us all than ever before. In Victorian days the Queen was so remote from those over whom she ruled that it caused relatively little controversy when, in the sorrow of her young widowhood, she withdrew almost completely from view for a quarter of a century, performing hardly any ceremonial duties and scarcely ever appearing in public. For Elizabeth II, such conduct would be unthinkable. But then Victoria, travelling incognito, could pass unrecognized among the vast majority of her subjects: the face of the present Queen, seen daily not only in stylized form on coins, banknotes and postage stamps but also in its more familar image on the newspaper page and the television screen, is better known, perhaps, than any other on earth. For most people of the nineteenth century, Victoria was Queen and Empress and that was that. For us, her great-great-granddaughter possesses a whole extra dimension. She is royal, certainly; but she is also a wife, a mother and a grandmother six times over. In many ways her life is astonishingly different from ours; in others, it is very much the same.

This unique combination of differences and similarities lies at the root of the perennial fascination which most of us feel, whether we admit it or not, about the Queen and her family – a fascination which affects not just those who actually recognize her as their ruler but extends to millions of others across the world, a tiny but none the less remarkable proportion of whom have actually seen and even met her – for few people on earth have travelled more widely than she has, or shaken more hands. Fascination, inevitably, breeds curiosity – a very natural desire to know more about this essentially ordinary family which finds itself placed, purely by reason of heredity and through no fault of its own, in a most extraordinary position. And it is partly to satisfy this curiosity that the SOVEREIGN exhibition has been conceived.

Partly, but by no means entirely: for SOVEREIGN is above all a celebration, intended to give proper recognition to the Queen's forty years on the throne. In the history of our monarchy, such a span is rare indeed. Of her thirty-nine predecessors since the Norman Conquest, only five – Henry III, Edward III, Elizabeth I, George III and Victoria – managed to equal such a figure, and, although Elizabeth II may be confidently expected to continue to reign over us for many more years yet, the forty-year mark provides us none the less with a good opportunity to offer her our congratulations, while at the same time looking back on the years since her accession in 1952 and trying to assess just how far they have brought us.

Thus the purpose of the exhibition was from the outset threefold: to celebrate, to inform and to take stock. How did we try to achieve it? The first thing, clearly, was to introduce our central figure. Who is she, and how was it that she suddenly became, at the age of just twenty-five, Elizabeth II, by the Grace of God, of the United Kingdom of Great Britain and Northern Ireland, and of her other Realms and Territories, Queen, Head of Commonwealth, Defender of the Faith? To answer this question we have provided, by way of a prologue, a family tree that traces her descent back almost exactly 1000 years to Ethelred the Unready, to-gether with a series of photographs, one of them taken during each year of her life up to 1952. It was on 6 February of that year, while she and her recently married husband were on an official visit to Kenya, that the news was brought to them of the sudden death of the father she loved, King George VI. They returned im-mediately, and those of us who are old enough to remember the day will, I am sure, be as moved as I was to see once again that famous picture of the small, black-clad figure emerging from the door of the aircraft while Sir Winston Chur-chill, Clement Attlee, Anthony Eden and others wait bare-headed at the bottom of the steps to receive her, their shoulders hunched against the winter wind.

And so, on 2 June 1953, the Queen proceeds to her coronation. Here, on public display for the first time in thirty-nine years, is the actual gown worn by her at the ceremony, together with her original blue velvet robe, gloves and prayer book, and the copes of the Archbishop of Canterbury and his fellow churchmen; while the video screen shows extracts from the original BBC television coverage of the occasion. Elizabeth II has embarked on her life as Queen – a life in which a naturally shy and retiring character finds herself unremittingly in the public gaze. The particular tasks that she is called upon to perform are the subject of a section which examines her various roles as respectively Head of State, of the Church and of the Armed Forces and as Fount of Honour. She is also Head of the Common-wealth: we see her on visits to Commonwealth countries, as well as to members of the European Community, the United States and elsewhere: by now there can be few leading statesmen anywhere in the world whom she has not met. But such luminaries she also receives on state visits to this country; and part of the great Palace dining-table, set with gold plate, crystal and porcelain for a state banquet, produces one of the most dazzling displays in the exhibition.

The next section, devoted to the Queen and the media, shows the astonishing development in the methods and approach of the press and television over four decades and leads us up to the great video wall on which we follow the Queen's reign up to the present day, not only through its principal events but also in the daily life of her subjects, tracing the enormous changes that we ourselves have undergone during the last forty years in our lives and lifestyles: the food we eat, the cars we drive, the clothes we wear, the songs we sing.

The Queen's own wardrobe is the theme of an important display, which shows a selection of her day and evening dresses through the years. This in turn introduces us to the last room of the Exhibition and the more private (or at least unofficial) aspects of the Queen's life. We look at her lasting love of racing and the turf and, by way of contrast, at the Royal Collection – perhaps the greatest private art collection in the world – which, thanks to her opening of the Queen's Gallery some twenty-five years ago, has been made infinitely more accessible to the general public than ever before.

Thus we come at last to the life of the Queen at home with the other members of the Royal Family. Here we have tried to evoke the atmosphere of the great royal country houses – Windsor, Sandringham and Balmoral – by re-creating a typical room in each.

How does one bring such an exhibition to an end? There is, after all, no natural conclusion: Elizabeth II is still Queen, and will surely remain Queen for as long as she lives. True, her Uncle Edward abdicated the throne, but he did so before the day set for his coronation. For crowned and anointed monarchs there can be no such escape: they cannot retire like the rest of us. Theirs is a life sentence, in which there are no holidays, no retirement. The work simply goes on: on whatever day you come to see SOVEREIGN, you may be sure that the Queen will be receiving the daily avalanche of Government Red Boxes, telegrams and letters, many of them requiring her immediate attention. That is why we have chosen to close our exhibition as we believe that she would wish us to close it, without fanfares or any artificial grand climax, but on a quieter note: that of dedication, obligation and commitment – the continuing purpose.

John Julius Norwich

A THOUSAND YEARS

Q UEEN ELIZABETH II is directly descended from Ethelred the Unready who was King of England one thousand years ago. Indeed her direct ancestry can be traced even further back to Egbert, who was King of Wessex in the ninth century.

This makes Britain's Royal House the oldest surviving dynasty in the world. Apart from the years 1649 to 1660 – when England temporarily became a republic – the line of succession has been continuous right up to the present day.

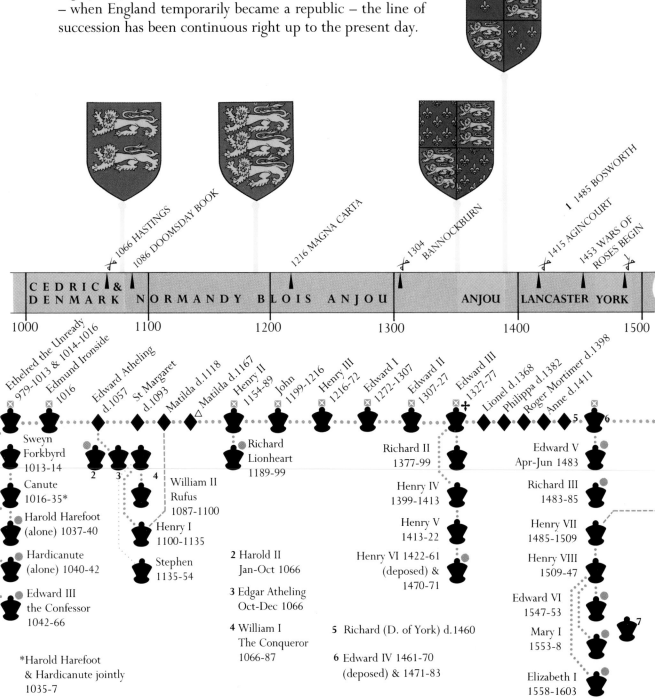

CEDRIC & DENMARK   NORMANDY   BLOIS   ANJOU   ANJOU   LANCASTER   YORK

1066 HASTINGS
1086 DOOMSDAY BOOK
1216 MAGNA CARTA
1304 BANNOCKBURN
1 1485 BOSWORTH
1415 AGINCOURT
1453 WARS OF ROSES BEGIN

1000   1100   1200   1300   1400   1500

Ethelred the Unready 979-1013 & 1014-1016
Edmund Ironside 1016
Edward Atheling d.1057
St Margaret d.1093
Matilda d.1118
Matilda d.1167
Henry II 1154-89
John 1199-1216
Henry III 1216-72
Edward I 1272-1307
Edward II 1307-27
Edward III 1327-77
Lionel d.1368
Philippa d.1382
Roger Mortimer d.1398
Anne d.1411

Sweyn Forkbyrd 1013-14

Canute 1016-35*

Harold Harefoot (alone) 1037-40

Hardicanute (alone) 1040-42

Edward III the Confessor 1042-66

William II Rufus 1087-1100

Henry I 1100-1135

Stephen 1135-54

Richard Lionheart 1189-99

Richard II 1377-99

Henry IV 1399-1413

Henry V 1413-22

Henry VI 1422-61 (deposed) & 1470-71

Edward V Apr-Jun 1483

Richard III 1483-85

Henry VII 1485-1509

Henry VIII 1509-47

Edward VI 1547-53

Mary I 1553-8

Elizabeth I 1558-1603

2 Harold II Jan-Oct 1066

3 Edgar Atheling Oct-Dec 1066

4 William I The Conqueror 1066-87

5 Richard (D. of York) d.1460

6 Edward IV 1461-70 (deposed) & 1471-83

*Harold Harefoot & Hardicanute jointly 1035-7

12

The Royal Line of Descent

This diagram traces the direct line of descent to Her Majesty
Queen Elizabeth II from Ethelred the Unready, King of England
one thousand years ago. The monarchs not in the direct line are
shown underneath.

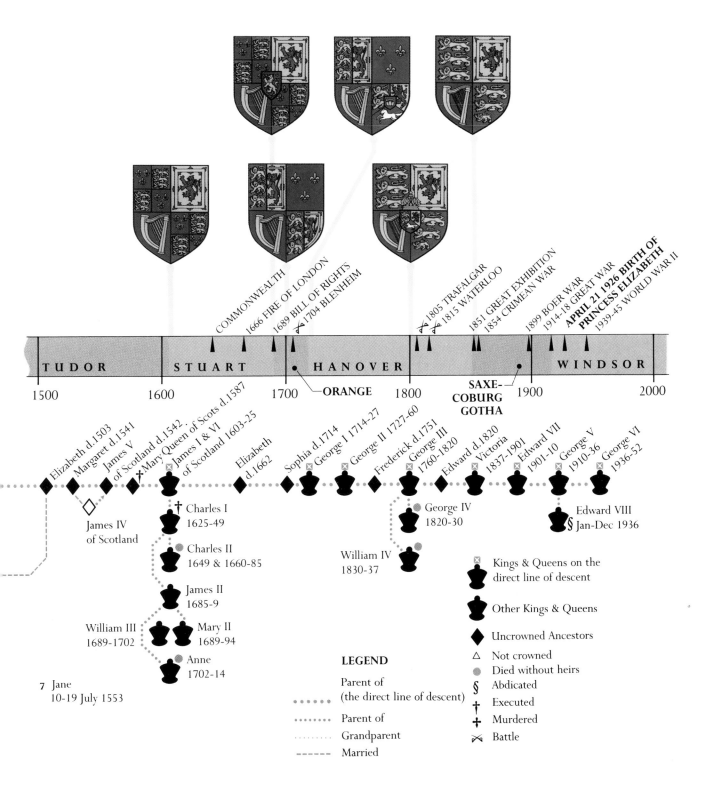

TUDOR   STUART   HANOVER   WINDSOR

1500   1600   1700   1800   1900   2000

ORANGE

SAXE-COBURG GOTHA

COMMONWEALTH
1666 FIRE OF LONDON
1689 BILL OF RIGHTS
1704 BLENHEIM
1805 TRAFALGAR
1815 WATERLOO
1851 GREAT EXHIBITION
1854 CRIMEAN WAR
1899 BOER WAR
1914-18 GREAT WAR
APRIL 21 1926 BIRTH OF PRINCESS ELIZABETH
1939-45 WORLD WAR II

Elizabeth d.1503
Margaret d.1541
James V of Scotland d.1542
Mary Queen of Scots d.1587
James I & VI of Scotland 1603-25
Elizabeth d.1662
Sophia d.1714
George I 1714-27
George II 1727-60
Frederick d.1751
George III 1760-1820
Edward d.1820
Victoria 1837-1901
Edward VII 1901-10
George V 1910-36
George VI 1936-52

James IV of Scotland

Charles I
1625-49

Charles II
1649 & 1660-85

James II
1685-9

William III
1689-1702

Mary II
1689-94

Anne
1702-14

George IV
1820-30

William IV
1830-37

Edward VIII
§ Jan-Dec 1936

7 Jane
10-19 July 1553

LEGEND

Parent of
(the direct line of descent)

Parent of

Grandparent

Married

Kings & Queens on the direct line of descent

Other Kings & Queens

Uncrowned Ancestors

△ Not crowned
● Died without heirs
§ Abdicated
† Executed
✝ Murdered
⚔ Battle

The ROYAL COAT OF ARMS

THE ROYAL ARMS ARE A TOKEN OF AUTHORITY. They are used in connection with those activities of administration and government which bear the Queen's name: British passports are just one example.

The layman, on first coming into contact with the language of heraldry, may be unsettled by terms such as arms, full achievement, supporters, crests, garters, helms, mantlings, coronets and compartments. Lions, and sometimes other creatures, are variously described. A rampant lion, for example, stands upright, ready to defend or attack; a couchant animal is one that is lying down. If it is lying with its head erect it is described as 'lodged'; a head on the ground or nestling upon paws is 'dormant'.

The current Royal Arms date from the reign of Queen Victoria; their individual elements are, however, much older and together tell us much about the history of the British monarchy.

Look first at the shield (the arms): the top left and bottom right quarters each bear three walking (passant) gold lions which stand for England. The top right quarter bears the rampant lion of Scotland; this emblem dates from the reign of Alexander II of Scotland (1214-49)

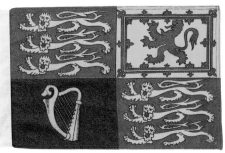

The Royal Standard
This is flown when the Queen is in residence in one of the royal palaces.

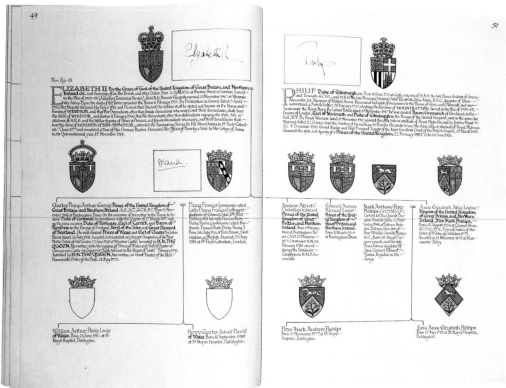

The Pedigree Book
Dating from the nineteenth century, the Pedigree Book illustrates the personal coats of arms of the Royal Family.

and became a part of the arms when James VI became James I of England in 1603. The bottom left quarter, bearing a harp, represents Ireland. This device became part of the arms during the reign of James I. The crest consists of a gold lion standing on a royal crown. The lion itself dates from Edward III (1327-77), but it gained its crown in the reign of Henry VIII (1509-47).

The garter surrounding the shield is that of the Most Noble Order of the Garter which was founded by Edward III. The supporter on the left is a lion rampant, on the right a unicorn. The lion dates from the time of Henry V (1413-22) and the unicorn from that of James I.

The motto 'Dieu et mon Droit' dates from the reign of Henry V.

The Royal Arms
The arms are on the central shield. On either side stand the supporters – a lion and a unicorn.

PRINCESS ELIZABETH

1926

1927

1928

1929

1930

1931

1932

1933

1934

1935

1936

1937

1938

1939

1940

1941

1942

1943

1944

1945

1946

1947

1948

1949

1950

1951

The KING IS DEAD

AS HEIR TO THE THRONE, Princess Elizabeth was carefully prepared in statecraft at the instigation of her father, George VI. The King himself had received no such schooling. His accession to the throne was a consequence of the unexpected abdication of his brother, Edward VIII.

None the less, George VI laid the foundations for the success of the modern monarchy by regaining his subjects' confidence in royal service and example. Crowned in 1937, he became Head of State at a time of international crisis, and led the country through five years of war and the long period of austerity that followed. The King displayed qualities of bravery, sympathy and leadership, and indeed stayed in London during the war to share the risks of the Blitz with his subjects. He established the George Cross and the George Medal for acts of civilian courage and he clawed back much of the royal prestige which had been lost during the short

reign of Edward VIII. After the war his reign was overshadowed by the tensions of the Cold War and the first moves in the transformation from British Empire to Commonwealth.

George VI died on 6 February 1952. His daughter, Princess Elizabeth, was in East Africa on the first leg of a Commonwealth tour and it was in Kenya – at the Sagana Lodge in the Aberdare Game Reserve – that she became Queen.

The return of Queen Elizabeth to London on 7 February 1952 was caught in one of the most famous photographs of her reign. The picture captures her alone, young and dressed in mourning, descending the steps of the BOAC Stratocruiser to be greeted by a line of black-clad figures, their heads bare and bowed – the senior politicians of the country, led by Winston Churchill.

Elizabeth Longford, the distinguished biographer, describes this period in the Queen's life as containing a double grief – grief for her dead father, and grief too that her own carefree youth was over: henceforth affairs of state would dominate her life.

On 8 February Queen Elizabeth read her Declaration of Sovereignty to the Privy Council assembled at St James's Palace. Then the Proclamation of Accession was publicly proclaimed by heralds at the traditional places: St James's Palace, the Strand (site of the original Charing Cross), Temple Bar and the Royal Exchange in London and also Edinburgh, Windsor and York.

On 6 June 1952, the Queen decreed that her coronation should take place on 2 June 1953 and even as she spoke the machinery of Government and Church was preparing for this most exacting and complex of great ceremonies.

The King Is Dead
Queen Elizabeth II returns from Africa, 7 February 1952 (opposite top left). King George VI (opposite) lying in state in Westminster Hall. Nearly one million people filed through to pay their last respects.

George VI's Funeral
Queen Elizabeth II, Queen Elizabeth the Queen Mother, and Queen Mary, mother of King George VI, at his funeral, on 16 February, 1952 (right).

Ceremonial
to be observed at the Funeral of
His Late Majesty
King George the Sixth
of Blessed Memory
February 15th, 1952

The CORONATION

Preparations for the coronation excited everyone for months. The Festival of Britain had been fun but there had been little else to enliven a life made drear by rationing. The coronation generated gossip: commoners were delighted to read in their newspapers such snippets as 'Sandwiches could be carried in Coronets', and were intrigued by articles entitled 'If Someone in the Abbey Shouts "No!"'

London was gripped by coronation fever. Coach parties toured the coronation route; in Piccadilly Eros was given a gilded cage; and the Mall was spanned with gold and azure arches, beneath which hung glittering crowns.

For weeks the motley of nobility and clerics had practised their steps and their words for the coronation. The Queen herself had rehearsed the ceremony in the Ballroom of Buckingham Palace using white bed sheets tied together to replicate the train of her gown.

On coronation eve 30,000 people were bedded down, twelve abreast on each side of the Mall, armed with stools, spirit-stoves, blankets, gramophones, radios, tinned food, and even tarpaulins and rubber dinghies.

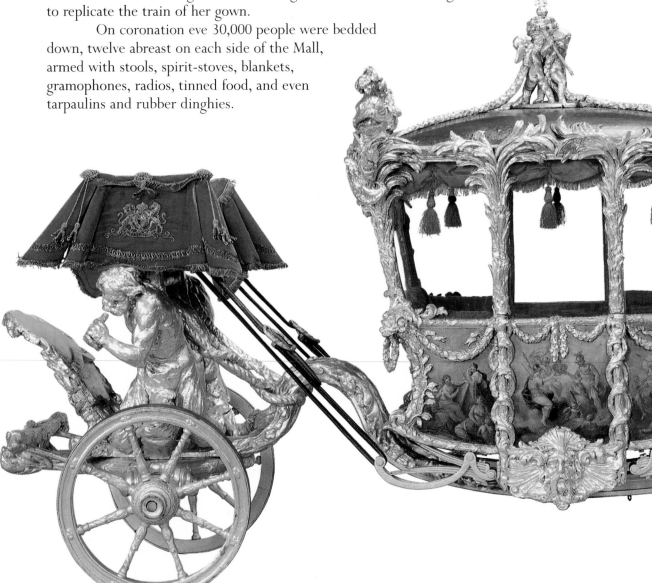

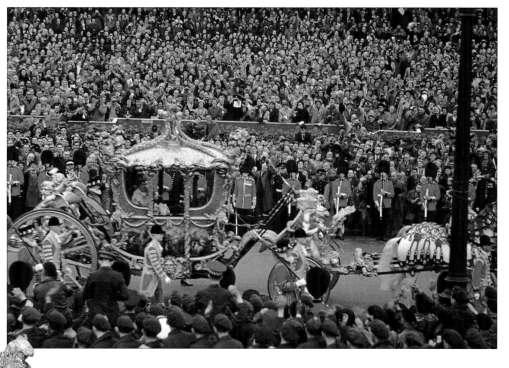

The Procession
The Queen travelled both to and from Westminster Abbey in the Gold State Coach. The coach was built in 1762 and weighs four tons. Eight horses draw the coach at walking pace.

The Coronation Coach
The exterior of the Gold State Coach is coated with gold leaf except for the panels painted by Giovanni Battista Cipriani. The structure consists of eight braces, shaped like palm trees. The roof is adorned with lions' heads and a crown supported by three cupids. Towards the front and back of the coach there is a pair of carved Sea Gods.

A Royal Coachman
The Royal Coachmen, dressed in Full State Livery, walked alongside the coach as it processed between Buckingham Palace and Westminster Abbey.

When the day dawned the crowds cheered everything that moved – starting with an early morning dustcart making a final clean sweep along the Mall. At last, shortly before 10.30 a.m., their vigil was rewarded with the first sight of the Gold State Coach. The gilding on the coach glistened in the pouring rain of that English summer morning and inside, amidst the crimson satin of the interior, sat Her Majesty the Queen.

The Gold State Coach, which had previously carried six sovereigns to their coronations, is an extraordinary confection of boldly carved lions' heads, tritons and cherubs, with side panels of paintings by Giovanni Battista Cipriani. It was made in 1762 for King George III and has been used for every coronation since William IV was crowned in 1831.

Eight thick-set Windsor Grey horses pulled the four-ton carapace along the coronation route to Westminster Abbey at a stately walking-pace, accompanied by a procession of Yeomen of the Guard, the Household Cavalry, the Royal Barge-master and, behind him, the Royal Watermen.

As the Queen entered the Abbey, over twenty million people, half the nation, watched on television: they had a better view than those guests who had waited for three hours in the Abbey.

The proceedings began with the recognition. Four times the Sovereign presented herself to the crowd in the Abbey: to east, to south, to west and to north. Four times the Archbishop of Canterbury declared, 'Sirs, I here present unto you Queen Elizabeth, your undoubted Queen. Wherefore all you who are come this day to do you homage and service, are you willing to do the same?'

Coronation Sketches
While the coronation was in progress, Cecil Beaton took the opportunity to sketch the various characters and scenes that surrounded him.

Cecil Beaton Portrait
The Queen is holding the Sovereign's Orb in her left hand, the Sceptre in her right.
She is wearing the Imperial State Crown, her Hartnell-designed coronation
dress, and the purple velvet Imperial Robe of State.

Four times the response was returned with a roar: 'God save Queen Elizabeth!' The recognition was followed by the coronation oath, in which the sovereign pledges to rule lawfully and with mercy.

The coronation then continued with the anointing, the central and most sacred part of this religious ceremony, accompanied by the choir singing Handel's anthem 'Zadok the Priest'. Sitting in King Edward's Chair, under a canopy to shield her from general view, the Sovereign was anointed, blessed and consecrated by the Archbishop, who dispensed the oil from the seventeenth-century Ampulla. (This is in the form of a golden eagle perched with wings outspread above a small gold well. The twelfth-century gold anointing spoon is one of the few items of coronation regalia to have survived Cromwell's purge of trumpery during the seventeenth century.)

Next came the investiture, for which the Queen put on a sleeveless white shift and a robe of gold cloth. She was then presented with the golden spurs (symbols of chivalry), the jewelled sword and the ar-mills – gold bracelets representing sincerity and wisdom.

The Great Sword of State
This dates from 1678 and was first used at the coronation of James II. It symbolizes the sovereign's power and is used at the State Opening of Parliament.

The Sovereign's Orb
The Orb, dating from 1661, was made for the coronation of Charles II. It is a hollow globe of gold, inset with rubies, sapphires and emeralds, which are surrounded by diamond clusters and bands of pearls. It is topped by a jewelled cross with an amethyst beneath.

The Imperial State Crown
Apart from the sapphire in the Maltese Cross, reputed to have come from the ring of Edward the Confessor, the four drop pearls below the cross, the Black Prince's ruby, the 104 carat Stuart sapphire, and the Second Star of Africa – the second largest cut diamond in the world – the crown contains four rubies, eleven emeralds, seventeen sapphires, 277 pearls and over 2,800 diamonds.

The Sceptre with the Cross.
First created for the coronation of Charles II, the sceptre was remodelled in 1910 to receive the largest cut diamond in the world – the Star of Africa – which weighs 530 carats.

After the Queen put on the royal robe, she received the orb (symbolizing both sovereign power and Christian rule); and finally the coronation ring, the coronation glove, the sceptre with the cross and the sceptre with the dove. Thus bedecked she sat, motionless, for the crowning itself. The Archbishop then raised St Edward's Crown into the air and then, slowly and gently, lowered it on to the Queen's head. At this moment the peers and peeresses placed their coronets upon their own heads to ringing shouts of 'God Save the Queen!'and a fanfare of trumpets. Queen Elizabeth II moved to her throne to receive the homage; first from the Archbishop of Canterbury, from her consort (the Duke of Edinburgh), and then senior peers of the realm, while all the Great Officers of the State took up positions round the throne.

When the ceremonial was finished, the Queen took Holy Communion and withdrew to St Edward's Chapel. Here she changed into the Robe of Purple Velvet and exchanged the heavy St Edward's Crown for the lighter Imperial State Crown, before starting off on the return journey to Buckingham Palace.

Later that day she appeared, still crowned, and surrounded by her family, on the balcony of Buckingham Palace. As the cheers of the crowds filled the vast open space in front of the Palace and extended up the Mall, they were almost drowned by the roar of twenty-four RAF fighters making their salute overhead.

The Ampulla and Anointing Spoon

These are the two oldest ceremonial objects used in the coronation ceremony. The main body of the eagle-shaped Ampulla, containing the holy oil used to anoint the sovereign, dates from the fourteenth century. It is thought that the spoon was in use as far back as 1199, at the coronation ceremony of King John.

The Coronation Prayerbook
This was bound in red morocco by
Sangorski and Sutcliffe and was
designed by Lynton Lamb.

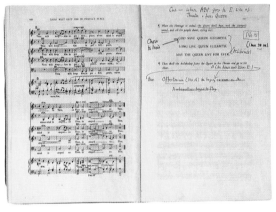

Walton Score
The score, of Walton's music played at
the coronation, was annotated in the
composer's own hand.

The Coronation Glove
Worn by the Queen in the
coronation ceremony, the glove
has the English, Scottish,
Welsh and Irish emblems
incorporated into
the embroidery.

The Purse
This contained one hundred
shillings with which the Queen
redeemed her sword after it had
been offered on the altar during
the coronation service and
hence had become the property
of the Abbey.

Millions more of her subjects pressed around the 2,700,000 television sets in every corner of the Kingdom.

It was the day that television came of age. The broadcasters rose to the challenge, and the planning that went into the coverage was as meticulous as that for the coronation itself. By being as unobtrusive as possible the BBC set the standards for all future television coverage of royal events: everyone, from Richard Dimbleby to the cameraman perched up high in Westminster Abbey, was attired in morning dress.

The Queen had insisted on the TV cameras, overruling her advisers who, in an excess of paternalism, had argued that the 'ordeal' of television would have placed too much strain upon her.

Churchill, her Prime Minister, had been surprised by her decision but, naturally, had given way to her wishes.

Now, in retrospect, we can see how right she was. Instinctively she saw from the start that television could link the public imaginatively and emotionally to their sovereign. In so doing, she provided those of her subjects lucky enough to see the coronation ceremony with an experience they will never forget.

Hugh Casson
Casson and Gooden were commissioned to design street
decorations for the capital. The sketch shows a train to be
painted on the side of Hungerford Bridge.

Hugh Casson
This massive coat of arms was among the impressive decorations designed to hang in Whitehall.

Richard Dimbleby
Richard Dimbleby, here outside Westminster Abbey, was the commentator inside during the coronation. He later commented; 'I'd never felt the strain of a public event so much.'

The Coronation on Camera
The presence of television cameras in Westminster Abbey, on the express orders of the Queen, broke all precedents and has since led to a number of other official occasions – such as both Houses of Parliament at work – appearing on the nations's television screens. It also gave millions of the Queen's subjects a rather better view of proceedings than the priviliged few who were in the Abbey.

The CORONATION DRESS

THE WHITE SATIN DRESS HAD SHORT SLEEVES, a fitted bodice and a full skirt adorned with emblems. Its creator, Norman Hartnell, has described how the Queen was unwilling to wear a gown bearing emblems of Great Britain without those of other connected nations. Thus the dress bore Canada's maple leaf, Australia's wattle flower, New Zealand's fern, South Africa's protea, the lotus flower of India and Ceylon (now Sri Lanka), and for Pakistan the crops of wheat, cotton and jute. Each motif was superbly crafted and embellished with pearls, diamonds, amethysts, crystals and gold and silver sequins. To support such an abundance of heavy embroidery the skirt was lined with taffeta reinforced with horsehair so that it should hang properly, without any distortion to the emblems.

**The Imperial
Robe of State**
The ermine cape, with
its purple velvet train,
is decorated with
gold lace and
filigree gold.

The Embroidery
The Coronation Dress
designed by Sir Norman
Hartnell was richly
embroidered with gold and
silver thread and precious
and semi-precious jewels.
The embroidery
incorporated motifs
representing all the
Queen's dominions.

The Coronation Dress
Hartnell's creation evolved through nine preliminary designs. Above is Hartnell's sketch and to the left the finished dress.

The QUEEN'S ESCORT

T HE HOUSEHOLD CAVALRY and the Foot Guards make up the Household Division. The Cavalry is made up of two regiments – the Life Guards and the Blues and Royals. The Foot Guards consist of five regiments – the Grenadier Guards, the Coldstream Guards, the Scots Guards, the Irish Guards and the Welsh Guards. The Queen inspects her guards at the sovereign's annual birthday parade, known as Trooping the Colour – the Colours being the flags of the regiment.

At the parade, which takes place at Horse Guards Parade off the Mall, the Queen is driven slowly in a horse-drawn carriage and closely inspects the ranks of the Foot Guards. She is returned to the saluting base and the massed bands put on an intricate display of marching and counter-marching in slow and quick time. Then a single drummer beats the 'Drummer's Call' signalling the start of Trooping the Colour. The Colour is handed from the Regimental Sergeant Major to the youngest ensign in the regiment and trooped along the ranks of guardsmen. This is exhausting work because the flag and pole are extremely heavy. To perform the task adequately the ensign will have spent some weeks beforehand in the gym. The

Trooping the Colour
The Queen, here pictured at the annual Trooping the Colour, is Colonel-in-Chief of all the Guards regiments.

Drum Major
On state occasions the Drum Major wears State Dress – a livery similar to that of the Household Cavalry.

soldiers then march past the Queen with the ensign lowering the Colour in salute as they pass her. The infantry soldiers are followed by the Cavalry and then the Queen takes her position at the head of her Guards and the procession marches up the Mall to Buckingham Palace.

Although the Guards are seen by the public as ceremonial functionaries, the men are of course trained soldiers. Indeed men from the regiments of the Household Division have served in nearly every conflict in which the British Army has been involved over the past 340 years.

The ceremonial duties of the Household Calvary include the provision of mounted escorts for the Queen and other members of the Royal family in state processions. The Foot Guards provide escorts on foot as well as being sentries at the royal palaces in London and Windsor.

A Scots Guard
Here shown in Guard Order
is a member of the regiment
first raised by Charles I
in 1642.

An Irish Guard
In recognition of their
bravery, Queen Victoria
formed her own regiment of
Irish Guards in 1900.

A Coldstream Guard
Here shown in Guard
Order. The regiment was
raised by Oliver Cromwell
in 1650.

A Welsh Guard
Here pictured in Winter
Guard, the Welsh Regiment
of Foot Guards was formed
in 1915 by George V.

A Constitutional Monarchy

Britain's royal house is the oldest dynasty in Europe and by far the most ancient of our political institutions. The Queen lies in a direct line of descent from Egbert, King of Wessex in the ninth century; and, apart from the years of 1649 to 1660, the descendants of Egbert have reigned continuously for nearly twelve hundred years.

From earliest times, sovereigns were expected to govern in the interests of their subjects. This notion was expressed in the coronation oaths of the early kings of Wessex, and later in Magna Carta, drawn up by the barons and accepted by King John on 19 June 1215 at Runnymede.

Amongst the sixty-three clauses of Magna Carta is the principle that no one should be imprisoned except by due process of law. This forms the basis of habeas corpus, which is still fundamental to our legal system. Magna Carta is the first major expression of constitutional monarchy, that the sovereign, no less than others, is subject to the rule of law.

In the seventeenth century, the Stuart kings put forward the theory of Divine Right, that the sovereign was subject only to God and not to the law. But this proved a deviation in our constitutional history, and in 1689, after James II had fled from London, Parliament reasserted itself by inviting William of Orange and his wife, Mary, to accept the crown. At the same time, Parliament presented William and Mary with a Declaration of Rights, which was eventually to become the Bill of Rights, affirming the liberties of the people. The Bill of Rights laid down that sovereigns could no longer interfere with elections, suspend laws of which they did not approve, levy money for their own use without parliamentary consent, nor interfere with the legal system. It was designed to ensure that Parliament could function free from royal intervention, and so it forms an important landmark in the path towards full parliamentary government.

Political developments in the eighteenth and nineteenth centuries did much to strengthen constitutional monarchy. The development of the system of a Cabinet enabled the government of the day to formulate a collective policy without interference from the sovereign; and, after 1717, George I, whose command of English was very limited, ceased to attend Cabinet meetings.

The growth of modern political parties in the nineteenth century offered the electorate a clear choice between alternative policies. The House of Commons came to reflect the decisions of the electors; and, in 1830, for the first time, a government, led by the Duke of Wellington, fell, even though it had the support of the King, because it had lost the confidence of the Commons.

At that time, however, the electorate was restricted mainly to male property-owners, and women were denied the vote. After the Reform Act of 1832,

The Magna Carta
Accepted by King John on 19 June 1215 at Runnymede, the
Magna Carta was the first document embodying the principle of
constitutional monarchy. It stated that the sovereign, no less
than others, was subject to the rule of law.

however, the franchise was gradually extended, until in 1928 all men and women over twenty-one were given the vote, so turning Britain into a fully fledged democracy. In 1969 the vote was extended to those over eighteen.

As democracy developed, so the sovereign was deprived of political power. Queen Victoria, who reigned from 1837 to 1901, was still able to intervene in politics, but George V (1910 to 1936) proved a model constitutional monarch. This tradition was continued by his son George VI and by Elizabeth II, who came to the throne in 1952. As a result, the ties which bind sovereign and people have grown continuously closer, and the monarchy has probably never stood so high in the affections of its subjects as it does today.

The sovereign, then, no longer enjoys political power. Indeed the essence of constitutional monarchy is that the sovereign must remain politically impartial. With very rare exceptions, public speeches and actions are undertaken only on the advice of ministers. This protects the sovereign from political involvement, and therefore from becoming a source of controversy.

But, although the sovereign lacks political power, he or she may, nevertheless, through royal influence, exert some impact upon the operation of government. It has been said that the sovereign in a constitutional monarchy has three rights: the right to be consulted, the right to encourage and the right to warn.

The Queen sees all government papers and holds a weekly audience with the Prime Minister, when both are in London. She has the right, and even the duty, to express her opinions on government policy. But her opinions must remain confidential, because it is ministers alone who are responsible for policy. For this reason, after having expressed her views, a constitutional monarch must, in the last resort, accede to the wishes of the government of the day.

A constitutional monarchy has the advantage that the sovereign is free from all party ties, and can act as a symbol of unity since he or she represents the people as a whole, rather than merely a section of society. The Queen has already been served by nine prime ministers, and has longer political experience than the vast majority of her subjects. But above all, a constitutional monarch remains, in the impersonal world of government, an essentially human symbol. It is for this reason that the constitutional monarchy has been so deeply valued by the British people for over three hundred years.

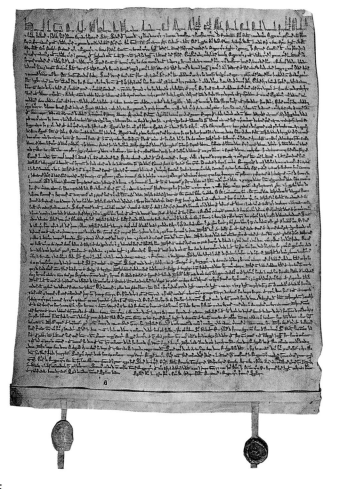

Vernon Bogdanor
Reader in Government, Oxford University, and fellow of Brasenose College.

FOUNT OF HONOUR

THE GARTER, THE ORDER OF THE THISTLE, the Order of Merit and the Royal Victorian Order are honours in the personal gift of the Queen. The other honours, starting with the British Empire Medal and ascending to peerages, are given in the name of the Crown but on the advice of the Prime Minister.

The Most Noble Order of The Garter, the oldest surviving order of chivalry in the world, was founded by King Edward III in 1348. The Order is select – only twenty-four Knights Companion at any one time. Each knight has a stall in St George's Chapel, Windsor, in which is placed his banner, helmet, crest, sword and stall plate bearing his coat of arms. On the death of a knight the banner and helmet are removed but the stall plate remains. Among those admitted to the Order by the Queen have been former prime ministers, heads of the Armed Forces, Chancellors of Universities, diplomats and explorers. The equivalent honour in Scotland is the Order of the Thistle.

The Royal Victorian Order, founded by Queen Victoria, is given by the sovereign as a mark of thanks for personal service. The Order of Merit is often given for the advancement of the arts, literature or science. It is restricted to twenty-four members. Among the recent holders have been the late sculptor Henry Moore, the medical researcher Professor Dorothy Hodgkin, the philosopher Sir Isaiah Berlin and Margaret Thatcher.

The Order of the Garter
The ceremony of the Most Noble Order of the Garter is held annually at St George's Chapel, Windsor.

The Thistle Badge
The gold badge contains the enamelled figure of St Andrew bearing his cross before him and the motto NEMO ME IMPUNE LACESSIT – no one harms me with impunity.

The Thistle Star
The Order of the Thistle is the highest honour in Scotland. It is thought to have been founded by James III of Scotland in the fifteenth century.

The Garter Star
The Most Noble Order of the Garter is the highest order of Chivalry in Britain; it was established by Edward III in 1348. The striated silver star displays the cross of St George and the Garter.

The George
The George (right) is a badge relating to the Order of the Garter. Introduced by Henry VII, it shows St George slaying the dragon.

The Lesser George
Smaller than the George, this is often worn on a blue sash (left).

The Garter
The motto on the Garter also appears on the Royal Coat of Arms: 'Shame on him who thinks this evil'.

A QUARTER OF THE WORLD

THE FIFTY INDEPENDENT COUNTRIES which together form the Commonwealth are spread around the world, across every continent and ocean. Its diversity in terms of population, language, culture, religious faith, race and lifestyles is unmatched by any other body – with the exception of the member states of the United Nations.

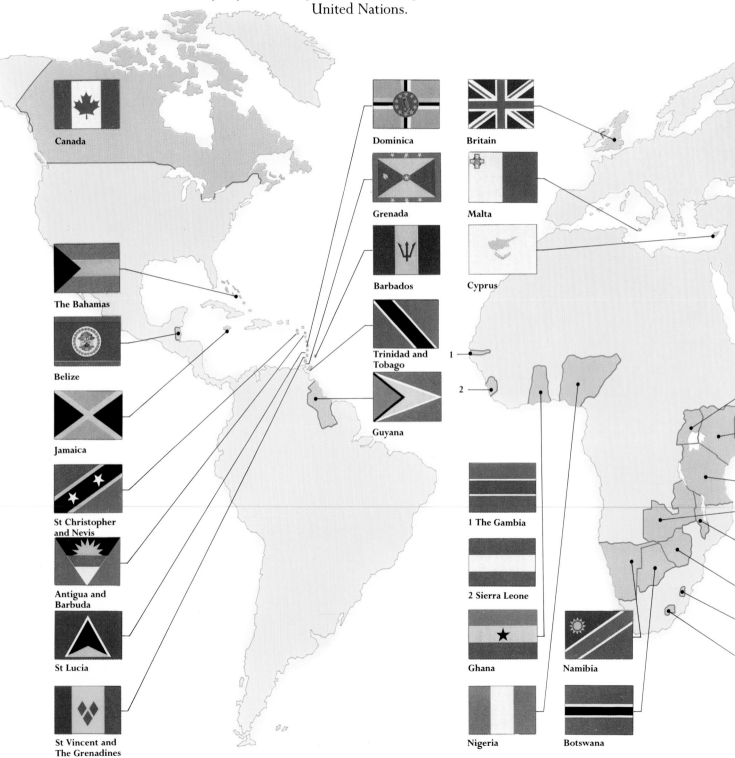

Canada

The Bahamas

Belize

Jamaica

St Christopher and Nevis

Antigua and Barbuda

St Lucia

St Vincent and The Grenadines

Dominica

Grenada

Barbados

Trinidad and Tobago

Guyana

Britain

Malta

Cyprus

1

2

1 The Gambia

2 Sierra Leone

Ghana

Namibia

Nigeria

Botswana

The biggest country, Canada, is over 450,000 times larger than the smallest, Nauru – one of the two special members of the Commonwealth – while India, the Commonwealth's most populous member, accounts for just under sixty per cent of the Commonwealth's total population, which in turn has over a quarter of the total population of the world.

The Commonwealth's origins go back to 1931, when the Statute of Westminster gave legal expression to the independence of the Dominions of Australia, Canada, New Zealand and South Africa. Since then it has gone from strength to strength. It welcomed its newest member, Namibia, in 1990.

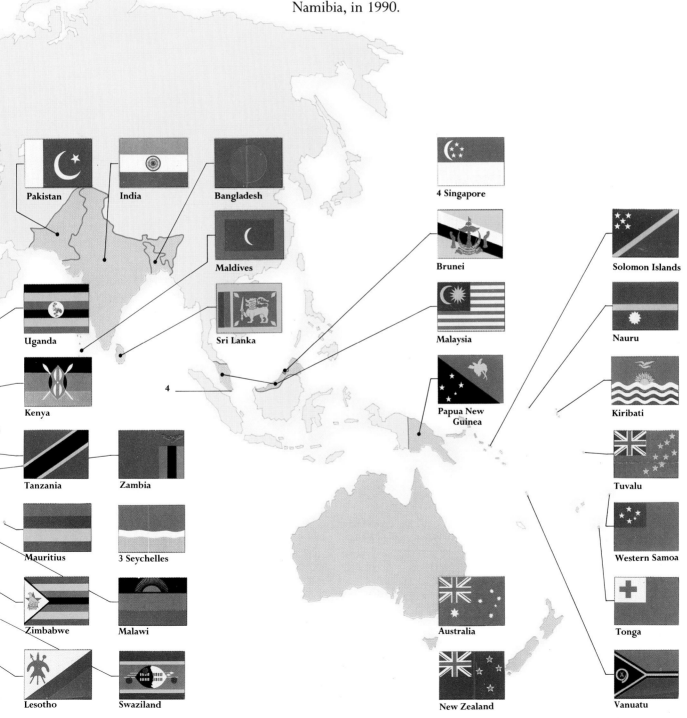

QUEEN AND COMMONWEALTH

THE QUEEN IS READILY ASSOCIATED with the Commonwealth for she is its Head, its elder statesman and has done so much to make this unique 'family' of nations work together. Many of her most important overseas tours have been to Commonwealth countries and she enjoys enormous prestige amongst all the member states. The Queen and the English language have been described as the mortar that holds the Commonwealth together. The Commonwealth relationship itself, although complex, is informal. The association has no constitution or charter. It is based only on principles of partnership and equality.

The Commonwealth of today has succeeded the British Commonwealth (a title discarded in the early 1950s), which in turn grew out of the British Empire. It is a voluntary association and at present over a quarter of the world's population live in the fifty independent countries which have come to make up the Commonwealth.

The official international organization of the Commonwealth, the

The Queen in Tuvalu
The Queen is here pictured being carried on a canoe during her tour to Australia and the Pacific Islands in October 1982. Tuvalu became a special member of the Commonwealth in 1978, the year it gained its independence.

Commonwealth Secretariat, has observer status at the United Nations and it is the engine of all the multilateral Commonwealth activities. It is through the Secretariat that the biennial Commonwealth conference is organized.

Every two years the heads of government of the Commonwealth meet and although the Queen does not attend the working sessions of this conference, she is usually in the host country where she meets privately with each of the Commonwealth countries' leaders. These meetings extend the friendship between Britain and individual member states of the Commonwealth but equally, because the Queen is politically impartial and very well-informed, her advice and encouragement can be most helpful. For example, the Queen is credited with having played an important informal role in the settlement of the Rhodesia (now Zimbabwe) question at the Commonwealth Heads of Government Meeting at Lusaka in 1979.

In recent years the Commonwealth has adopted a high profile on such issues as race and apartheid, and it is particularly concerned about the security of small states. After all, half of the member countries have a population of less than a million people and concern has long been expressed over the precariousness of their freedom, dependent as they are on a few products and trading partners while being vulnerable to external interference. Small states are assisted by other members of the Commonwealth in many fields, not least in ensuring their effective diplomatic representation.

Two of the oldest areas of Commonwealth collaboration are education and health. Each year thousands of students get the chance through scholarship and other schemes to study at the world's centres of educational excellence, while the Royal Commonwealth Society for the Blind, which runs the world's largest sight restoration programme, gives sight back to 100,000 people a year.

In recognition of the unique role that the Queen has played in encouraging the Commonwealth's modern spirit of equality and partnership, a new mace has been designed, commissioned by the Royal Anniversary Trust. Made from 18 carat gold originating from many different Commonwealth sources, it incorporates the flags of each of the Commonwealth nations. It is accompanied by a set of fifty gold-plated toasting goblets, given by and bearing the arms of each nation of the Commonwealth.

The Queen in New Zealand

New Zealand was one of the first countries to join the Commonwealth in 1931 and since her coronation the Queen has made official visits to the country on eight separate occasions. Here she is pictured with the Maoris, descendants of Polynesian voyagers who migrated in successive waves from the sixteenth century onwards – well before the European settlers arrived.

$\mathscr{A}$ $\mathscr{S}$TATE BANQUET

$\mathbb{S}$TATE VISITS BETWEEN NATIONS are a part of the world of international diplomacy. It would, of course, be unthinkable for the Queen to extend an invitation and be turned down. So the British Foreign and Commonwealth Office takes the first step in suggesting the overseas head of state to be invited and, if the Queen agrees, the suggestion is then explored unofficially with representatives of that country. Only when the reaction is positive is an official invitation issued.

The state banquet, usually given on the evening of the first day of the visit, either at Buckingham Palace or Windsor Castle, is an important public display of friendship or respect between the two nations.

The organization of such a banquet is formidable, especially as the word 'Royal' has become a synonym for excellence. Having a long tradition of ceremony

A Royal Banquet
A royal banquet is a carefully rehearsed occasion enhanced
by flowers, music and, of course, magnificent ornaments.

is an advantage, however, in that the choreography remains essentially the same. A state banquet is a repeat performance with every detail honed to a fine art.

Nevertheless, each banquet takes several months of planning: from the preliminary discussions between the Master of the Household, Her Majesty's Private Secretary and the Foreign and Commonwealth Office about invitations, to the budget created by the Keeper of the Privy Purse – for the food, wine, music and decorations. The Yeomen of the Pantries are briefed as to the plate, glass and china to be used. It then takes a full two days just to lay the tables.

Of the many dinner services in the Royal Collection's European ceramics, the Sèvres ware is probably the most spectacular. The major part of the royal collection of Sèvres was acquired between 1783 and 1829, the years when the French national porcelain factory was at the forefront of European ceramic producion. In 1947 the Queen – then Princess Elizabeth – was presented with a modern Sèvres dinner service as a present from France.

A Place at Table
A typical place setting for a royal banquet. The glass is from Stourbridge and the cruets were modelled by Paul Storr in 1813.

A Banquet Setting
The table setting is for four courses – soup, fish, meat and dessert.
There are one glass for sherry, three for wine, one for water and one for port.

The most modern example of Sèvres ware, which has appeared for display on the occasion of a state visit from France, is a large porcelain grasshopper given in 1972 by the President of France to the Duke of Edinburgh.

English ware also features strongly – Minton, Spode, Wedgwood and Flight and Barr. At a state banquet, where there are side tables bearing silver gilt and porcelain for decoration, there might also be a selection of nineteenth-century neo-rococo Rockingham pottery with exuberant flower decorations.

For a banquet at Buckingham Palace guests gather in the Picture Gallery, where they are received by the Queen and the visiting head of state, before taking their seats at the U-shaped dining-table in the Ballroom. Then all stand as the Queen's procession enters, led by herself and the visiting head of state, and preceded by both the Lord Chamberlain and the Lord Steward, walking backwards.

The Queen, her principle guests and other members of her procession sit at the top of the U-shaped table, while the remaining 160 or so guests are distributed according to a seating plan finely tuned to the nuances of diplomacy and rank. Guests are waited upon by footmen in a livery of scarlet and gold, assisted by pages in black and gold.

Waterloo Chamber
This imposing room, at Windsor Castle, is often used
for banquets and other state occasions.

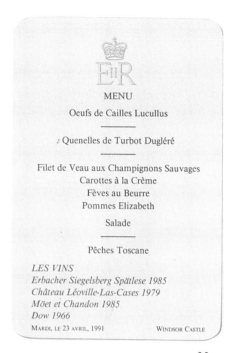

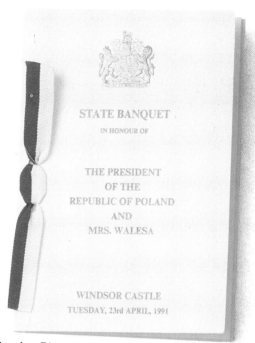

EⅡR
MENU
Oeufs de Cailles Lucullus

Quenelles de Turbot Dugléré

Filet de Veau aux Champignons Sauvages
Carottes à la Crème
Fèves au Beurre
Pommes Elizabeth

Salade

Pêches Toscane

LES VINS
Erbacher Siegelsberg Spätlese 1985
Château Léoville-Las-Cases 1979
Möet et Chandon 1985
Dow 1966
MARDI, LE 23 AVRIL, 1991   WINDSOR CASTLE

STATE BANQUET
IN HONOUR OF

THE PRESIDENT
OF THE
REPUBLIC OF POLAND
AND
MRS. WALESA

WINDSOR CASTLE
TUESDAY, 23rd APRIL, 1991

Menu and Seating Plan
A banquet in honour of Lech Walesa and his wife.

Every item on the table will have been measured into place, and even the serving of each course is carefully regulated by means of a signalling system of lights so as to ensure perfect co-ordination.

Flowers – some from the greenhouses at Windsor – in gilded vases and candles in silver gilt candelabra decorate a table already lavishly endowed with golden tableware. This comes in a variety of forms. The mustard might be held aloft by mermaids and Neptunes, or the salt carried in a gilded panier, on the back of a golden donkey.

Dessert Stand
Made by Paul Storr, this dessert stand has two tritons supporting a shell. The circular base is raised on four out-turned scroll, grape and shell feet.

Triton Salt
The silver gilt Triton Salt is another piece by Paul Storr, Britain's leading Regency silversmith, in 1813.

Donkey Salt
This Salt, also by Paul Storr, was made in 1810. It is said to be one of the Queen's favourites.

Main courses are eaten from gold plate, desserts from Minton, or one of the other fine ceramic services. Wine is served in fluted cut glass from Stourbridge. The banquet is accompanied by light music played by military musicians in the orchestra gallery.

At the end of dinner the Queen makes a speech, to which the visiting head of state replies, and proposes the Queen's health. Then twelve pipers enter and march around the table before playing a strathspey and reel. They then perform another march around the table and exit.

The Queen and her procession then leave as they entered, followed shortly afterwards by the other guests, who withdraw to a nearby State Room for coffee and liqueurs.

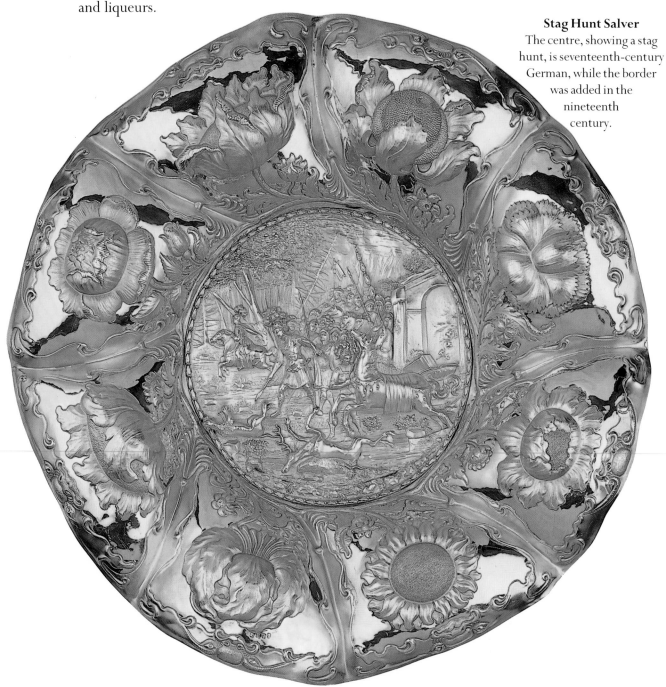

Stag Hunt Salver
The centre, showing a stag hunt, is seventeenth-century German, while the border was added in the nineteenth century.

Tournai Porcelain
These two delightful plates (above
and left) were part of a service of
1,603 pieces – now dispersed –
commissioned in 1787 by Philippe,
Duc d'Orléans.

Minton
This plate is from a service
commissioned from the Minton
factory by Queen Victoria.

Wine Flagon
This richly chased flagon (above) incorporates
the emblems of England, Scotland and Wales. It
was made by John Bridge in 1828.

Candle Sconce
The relief on this sconce (right) depicts the
Judgement of Solomon.

ANATOMY OF A JOURNEY

WITH THE EXCEPTION OF 1955, when her only official overseas visit was to Norway, the Queen has made at least two official trips abroad every year since her accession to the throne. Many of these have lasted for weeks, encompassing a number of different countries, and so have required meticulous organization, with every forseeable problem dealt with in advance.

In 1986 the Queen visited China. Politically it was one of her most important state visits as it was seen by the Governments of both countries as cementing the Hong Kong agreement which provided for the return of Hong Kong to Chinese rule in 1997. China was then going through a period of liberalization.

As with all the Queen's overseas tours, it needed elaborate planning, a process which began back in July 1984 when the invitation was received from Deng Xiaoping. The following year the Queen's Deputy Private Secretary visited China for a preliminary reconnaissance to consider the places and people she should visit. A provisional itinerary was then submitted to the Queen and the Duke of Edinburgh and, once the draft had been agreed, the work began, sorting out all the details that ensure the smooth running and success of a royal visit.

The Blue Book

Every state visit has its own Blue Book, detailing the itinerary of the Queen and the Duke of Edinburgh. Months of planning lie behind its creation.

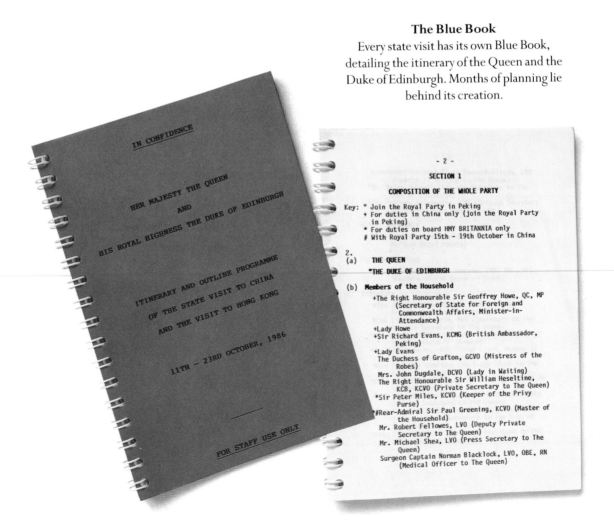

The Queen in China
The Queen and Li Xiamian, President of
China, exchange formal toasts.
This historic moment symbolized a
significant *rapprochement* between
two nations at opposite ends
of the political spectrum.

Part of the mystique of a royal visit is its reliability – that hardly anything ever does go wrong. One of the secrets of this enviable record is the Blue Book, which contains the full itinerary of a visit, with exact times for every stage of every day's activity. If the Book states that the Queen will be at such and such a place at 9.35 am and will depart by aeroplane at 9.57 am, then she is and she does. Every conceivable detail is worked out in advance, with nothing left to chance. In the case of the China visit the first draft of the Blue Book was ready at the end of November 1985 – nearly a year before the Queen's visit actually took place.

A long tour needs a sizeable support staff, upwards of forty people – some, such as the Private and Press Secretaries, to assist the Queen in making the visit a diplomatic success, other members of the Queen's Household to look after all the practical arrangements.

CHINA

Saturday 11th October

THE QUEEN

| 5.00 p.m. | Leave London Airport in British Airways Tristar. (8 hours flying time) GMT + 1 |
| | Dress: L.S. |

Sunday 12th October

4.00 a.m.	Arrive Muscat. GMT + 4
5.00 a.m.	Leave Muscat. (8 hours flying time)
[3.25 p.m.	Sir Geoffrey and Lady Howe arrive from Hong Kong.]

THE DUKE OF EDINBURGH

| 4.30 p.m. | Arrive Peking Airport in Queen's Flight 146. |

THE QUEEN

5.00 p.m.	Arrive Peking. GMT + 8
	The Duke of Edinburgh boards the aircraft, accompanied by Mr. Wu Minglian (Director of Protocol, Ministry of Foreign Affairs) and Sir Richard Evans (British Ambassador, Peking).
	Presentations to representatives of Chinese Government (4).
5.05 p.m.	Leave airport by car. (24 km)
5.45 p.m.	Arrive Diaoyutai State Guest House, Villa 18
later	Private Dinner.
[6.00 p.m.	The Master of the Household and Party leave Peking Airport in British Airways Tristar.
7.50 p.m.	Arrive Shanghai Airport
	Board HMY BRITANNIA.]

Monday 13th October

| 9.50 a.m. | Leave by car. (8 km) |
| | Dress: L.S. |

CHINA

Monday 13th October (continued)

10.00 a.m.	Arrive Tian'anmen Square.
	Welcome Ceremony.
	Presentation of Chinese Senior Officials and Royal Household.
	Inspect Guard of Honour.
	Welcome by children.
	Presentation of Embassy staff.
	March-past.
10.15 a.m.	Enter Great Hall of the People.
	Formal talks, accompanied by The Duke of Edinburgh, with President Li Xiannian.
10.45 a.m. (approx)	Leave by car.
10.55 a.m.	Arrive State Guest House, Villa 18.
11.15 a.m. – 12.05 p.m.	Press Reception (160) at Villa 18.
	Private Lunch.
1.30 p.m.	Leave by car. (8 km)
1.40 p.m.	Visit Palace Museum (Forbidden City).
2.40 p.m.	Leave by car. (3 km)
2.50 p.m.	Visit Temple of Heaven.
3.40 p.m.	Leave by car. (6 km)
4.00 p.m.	Arrive British Embassy.
	Received by Sir Richard and Lady Evans.
	Plant tree in Residence garden.
	Sign Visitors' book.
4.05 p.m.	Retire.
4.10 p.m.	Meet Commonwealth Ambassadors (18).
	Photograph.

- 10 -

- 11 -

These are daunting. When the Queen left for China in October 1986, her luggage included nine briefcases, five personal stationery boxes, two trunks containing Her Majesty's despatch boxes, twelve boxes of the Queen's gifts to the Head of State, eight boxes of word processors and printers, and four tons of Master of the Household's luggage and the Queen's personal luggage.

The large number of public engagements carried out in the course of a royal visit imposes a very strenuous schedule on everyone. In a large country like China, vast distances had to be covered between engagements: sometimes there were two air flights a day, each of over two hours' duration.

Most overseas travel is by air, sometimes on an aircraft of the Queen's Flight, sometimes on an aircraft chartered from a commercial airline. The most regal transport is perhaps the Royal Yacht *Britannia*, which was used on the visit to China. This lovely, dark-blue-hulled ship serves as a floating palace in which the Queen can offer hospitality to her hosts and hold gatherings to promote British industry abroad. Most ships are noisy with the barked commands of officers, the clatter of feet and the percussive sounds of bells and alarms; not so *Britannia*. Most commands are given via signals and the sailors wear plimsolls. The only bells are for security or fire warnings. *Britannia*, however, has also been used for less ceremonial purposes: indeed nine months before going to China it was used to rescue over a thousand British refugees and other expatriates from Aden, when civil war broke out in South Yemen.

The Terracotta Army
While the Queen was in China, she visited some of the
country's historic wonders including the Terracotta Army at
Xian. She also visited the Great Wall and sailed down the
Yangtze River.

A Banquet Abroad
As in Britain, banquets are an
essential element of official
hospitality overseas.

During the course of her visit to China the Queen went to Beijing, the capital (formerly known as Peking), Shanghai and Canton, saw the Great Wall of China, the Forbidden City of the Emperors and sailed along the Yangtze River. John Osman, who was covering the visit for the BBC, said he found it both memorable and exhausting, as day after day the itinerary demanded travel from one far-flung corner of China to the other. In that same year the Queen had also toured Nepal, New Zealand and Australia.

Throughout the world the Queen is a valued visitor, as her integrity and unique world standing confer recognition on her host. For this reason a state visit is never undertaken lightly; all political implications must be carefully evaluated before an invitation is accepted. Thus although the Queen is one of the most well-travelled heads of state in the world she cannot, for both practical and diplomatic reasons, accede to every request for her to visit a country abroad.

In 1992 the Queen's schedule is as busy as ever; on top of all her domestic engagements she is visiting Australia in February, Malta in May, France in June, Canada in July and Germany in October.

Guard of Honour
Accompanied by President Li Xiamian, the Queen
inspects the Guard of Honour – a traditional courtesy of the
state visit.

*D*RESSING TO BE SEEN

T HE QUEEN, IT IS SAID, does not judge people by their dress, but by whether they are neat and tidy. She is also reported as being largely indifferent to fashion, and when pursuing her private outdoor interests she is most likely to be wearing a waterproof jacket and a headscarf. None the less, her varied and numerous public engagements mean that she takes her choice of clothes seriously as a practical element in doing her job. After all, many more people see the Queen from a distance than have an opportunity to talk to her, and she wants her clothes to enhance their view of her.

The Queen has steered a careful sartorial line – neither drab nor ostentatious. Where the occasion warrants it and expectations are not to be dashed, she will commission a special garment. Her designers have included Sir Norman Hartnell, Sir Hardy Amies, Ian Thomas and John Anderson. They, together with the Queen's dresser – Margaret 'Bobo' MacDonald – have created her style.

This style is a mixture of 1950s and 1970s fashion. Some people have observed that had the Queen had a French rather than an English dresser, then she would have been a leader of fashion. But in modern times it is not appropriate for heads of state to be fashion plates, and in any case the Queen has developed her own style – consistent but not boring.

Betty Reeves, Maud Beard, Hardy Amies, Mr. Leonard setting off for Buckingham Palace 1954

Modern but Modest
Hardy Amies had shortened his Sovereign's dress as far as he dared.

The Albums

After each royal tour Hardy Amies and his staff compiled a scrapbook of photographs and press cuttings of the Queen in her various outfits, which they then annotated. Shown here are pages featuring the Australia tour of 1973, Japan in 1975, the Queen's Silver Jubilee tour in 1977 and her visit to the USA in 1983.

Simply by being who she is the Queen creates an effect of subdued drama and this is often heightened by the vivid colours she wears. Lady Longford relates, 'In being photographed with her Yeomen of the Guard she chose a red for her dress that must have been dyed exactly to match theirs.'

The Queen likes bright colours which make her stand out; she is fortunate because her colouring allows her to wear difficult hues such as yellow and lime green. Her clothes have to be comfortable, suitable for the occasion and easy to change. Her hats should not hide her face, her shoes should be elegant and give added height, and her gloves serve to protect her hands. Moreover her clothes and accessories are designed collectively so that the emphasis is on the overall impression.

The Queen uses British suppliers for her clothes and accessories – a royal convention that is both patriotic and practical.

Norman Hartnell
This embroidery was for the State Evening Dress
sketched right, first worn by the Queen in 1957.

Norman Hartnell
The beautiful lace dress to the left was designed for the Queen's visit to the Vatican in 1961. The lace is mounted on stiff net, and flowers from the lace were appliquéd round the black-net yoke and edged the black tulle veil. The white dress to the right, embroidered with silver thread, diamonds and emerald drop beads, was for Iran, 1961. Below, with samples attached, are sketches for day outfits, prepared for the Queen's approval.

It means that consultations and fittings are easier. One can also expect discretion from suppliers who are also one's subjects.

Different designers for the Queen are associated with different aspects of her wardrobe. Hartnell's vision was romantic. He almost out-Frenched the French in the art of haute couture. He designed many of the fabulous evening gowns that the Queen wore at state functions in the early years of her reign. Hardy Amies, a master of the tailored outfit, has created much of the Queen's daywear: soft, fluid suits and low-waisted dresses which cover the knee. Ian Thomas, who used to work for Sir Norman Hartnell, now designs daywear for the Queen but, like his mentor, sometimes lets himself go with glamorous richly embroidered gowns where the occasion demands it.

A designer who is given a brief for, say, a royal tour is expected to provide appropriate changes of clothing that take account of the different climates to be encountered. Drawings are submitted to the Queen with full portraits to show the total effect. A visit to the Palace is normally made with further sketches and fabric samples and the Queen usually takes two or three days to consider the suitability of the designs – and the costs. The Queen is not parsimonious in providing clothes for 'the job' but she is also not profligate and outfits are often worn many times.

As Elizabeth Longford says, the Queen's aim is to be recognized by her subjects rather than copied by them.

Rayne

Rayne were awarded their first Royal Warrant in 1930. They presently make shoes and handbags for the Queen, the Queen Mother, Princess Margaret and the Princess of Wales.

The Queen's Milliner
Some pages from the scrapbook in which Simone Mirman, who made the Queen's hats for over thirty years, recorded her most successful designs. These hats were created for the Queen's 1977 Jubilee Commonwealth Tour.

The QUEEN AND THE MEDIA

P ERHAPS NOT SURPRISINGLY, relations between the media and the monarchy have changed dramatically since 1952. When Princess Elizabeth came to the throne, newspaper reporters assigned to royal duties were expected to wear bowler hats. Workmen who watched the coronation on tiny television screens in pubs felt impelled to doff their caps in respect.

In 1964, thirty per cent of those questioned believed that the Queen had been specially chosen by God, and most people still agreed with what the constitutional expert Walter Bagehot had written in 1867: 'Above all this our royalty is to be reverenced. In its mystery is its life. We must not let daylight in upon magic.'

Since the 1950s television has let in quite a bit of light, and Fleet Street has done its best to illuminate a few corners.

Not many people in high places foresaw television as the great communicator that it has become – though the Queen did. She insisted on her coronation being televised when some, including her Prime Minister, Winston Churchill, were at first hesitant. 'What arguments will remain for refusing TV facilities of e.g. royal funerals or weddings, religious services, or even proceedings in the House of Commons?' argued Sir Norman Brook, Secretary of the Cabinet, in a memorandum.

Up until the mid-sixties, newspapers and radio were the main outlet for royal pronouncements – the word 'news' itself had slightly suspicious undertones of sensationalism in some Palace minds. Respect and control were taken to extraordinary lengths, by both public and Palace alike. Godfrey Talbot, the BBC's court correspondent, was criticized by a listener for referring to Her Majesty as 'she'. And when the Duke of Gloucester – brother of George VI – died at a slightly inconvenient hour of the evening, the Press Association's court correspondent was asked not to spread the news until the following morning.

However, fifteen years into the reign of Queen Elizabeth, attitudes had already begun to change. Many young people now regarded the Queen as an 'arch square', declared the *Sunday Telegraph*, predicting in an editorial that the monarchy might be 'swallowed in a great and growing yawn'.

Prince Philip realized that a young queen and a young family had been infinitely more newsworthy and amusing, but now that the Queen and he were approaching middle age, 'people either can't stand us, or think we're all right – I dare say when we're really ancient there might be a bit more reverence again.'

For many years the Queen's Press Secretary was a former Royal Naval commander, who retired from his post with the warning that 'if there comes a time when the British monarchy needs a real public-relations officer, the institution of monarchy in this country will be in serious decline.'

His successor, an Australian, was concerned that the Royal Family were no longer 'rounded' figures in the public imagination and was largely responsible for advising the Queen to co-operate on *Royal Family*, the documentary film shown in 1969 to an audience of forty million worldwide.

Since then the Royal Family as a whole has tended towards television as opposed to newspapers and magazines when granting interviews and insights –

mainly, one suspects, because they have more control over television appearances, and also because royal charities usually benefit financially from sales of programmes. But it is interesting to note that the Queen waited twenty-two years before agreeing to participate in the making of another film about her working life – *Elizabeth R*, shown on BBC 1 this year.

Fleet Street's response to partial eclipse by television over the years has been to search out the stories that television couldn't get, or wouldn't touch.

The Queen – as the Lords would like to see her, by Cummings

Her Majesty on the way to open Parliament (ceremony delayed owing to traffic in Oxford Street).

Buckingham Palace exchanged for a more democratic home...

State banquet to foreign prime minister in strictly 'non-tweedy' surroundings...

All Her speeches to be written by a committee composed of Sir Winston, Bertrand Russell, Evelyn Waugh & T.S. Eliot.

And, of course, the speeches to be sung by a prima donna of the opera for Her.

And in so doing, help to assuage the voracious appetite of millions of readers for royal stories.

From the seventies onwards the tabloids began building up a soap-opera scenario around individual members of the Royal Family – aided to some extent by the real-life behaviour of some of the younger members.

The courtship, engagement and marriage of the Prince and Princess of Wales provided endless opportunities for speculation, snatched pictures and increased circulation.

The famous photographs of a pregnant Princess Diana in a bikini in the Bahamas – 'Bahama Mama', headlined the Sun – were condemned by Buckingham Palace as being 'in the worst possible taste'. But they put on sales.

The Queen by nature is a tolerant and pragmatic person, but she cannot abide invasion of privacy. Only weeks before the bikini incident she had taken the very unusual step of inviting all the national newspaper editors to Buckingham Palace to warn of the very real danger to Princess Diana's health through continuous harassment.

Since that time – the early eighties – relations between press and the Palace have remained guarded but on the whole good. Nowadays the Queen herself figures less in television reports and in the newspapers than some other members of her family – though one suspects the position may have changed markedly by the conclusion of a year of celebrations of her fortieth anniversary as Queen.

Although it is sometimes accused of trivializing the Royal Family, Fleet Street has remained for forty years a strong supporter and genuine admirer of the Queen herself, both as a person and as the focal point of the nation. Ironically it is television, the new influence, with programmes such as *Spitting Image* and *Pallas*, which has started to mock and sometimes be more than a little cruel, all in the name of satire and good fun.

Through it all the Queen sails calmly on, untroubled but keenly aware. As well as anyone, she realizes that the institution that she represents relies quite heavily on media which can choose to be supportive or destructive. And which is never far away.

Douglas Keay

The JOKE'S ON US

I N SOME COUNTRIES in Europe you can be fined or imprisoned for abusing the national flag – we print ours on tea towels and biscuit tins. In many countries teasing the head of state in newspaper cartoons is simply not allowed. In Britain the husband of the Head of State collects the originals of cartoons about his family and hangs them in the royal palaces. This selection of cartoons focuses on the Silver Jubilee (below), the Duke of Edinburgh himself (opposite top), and royal visits abroad (opposite bottom).

'I can see 'em now. "Oo! A little silver gravy boat, just what we wanted".'

'You are supposed to hold your street party in your street not hers.'

'As the only nationalized industry that makes a fortune why not get Her Majesty to celebrate her jubilee EVERY year?'

'They wondered if you do
guided tours, Sir.'

'Hang on Sir, my mistake, you're Admiral of the Fleet today.

'Philip – please stop
calling me Fred'

'...But where in the bloody attic?'

$\mathscr{S}$TAMPS

$\mathscr{S}$TAMP COLLECTING is one of Britain's most popular hobbies and Buckingham Palace houses the world's largest collection of British and Commonwealth Stamps. Indeed King George V was not only an enthusiastic philatelist, he was also particularly knowledgeable.

Since 1840 every definitive issue of a stamp has carried the portrait of the monarch – definitive meaning stamps that are permanently on sale as distinct from special issues. In 1952, with the accession of Queen Elizabeth II, it was decided to experiment with a photographic portrait instead of the traditional drawing.

A few days after her accession, portrait photographs of the Queen in three-quarter and profile views were taken by Dorothy Wilding Ltd. One of the three-quarter views was sent to the artist Edmund Dulac from which he made various drawn portraits. In April 1952 a fresh set of photographs was commissioned and in July it was decided to adopt one of these rather than a drawn portrait by Dulac. Meanwhile nine artists had been shortlisted by the Postmaster

Penny Blacks
Introduced in 1840, the Penny Black remains an inspiration to modern designers. However, having a largely black hue to a stamp makes franking harder – and forgery easier.

The Wilding Portrait
This was the basis for all stamp design from December 1952 to 1965. To the right is an early design by Enid Marx.

General to design the frames of the stamps. Each artist was given the same Dorothy Wilding portrait to work with. The Queen approved five designs: by Enid Marx, M.C.Farrar-Bell, Mary Adshead, Edmund Dulac and G.Knipe.

The designs by Enid Marx for the 1½d and M. C. Farrar-Bell's 2½d were issued in December 1952. Other designs followed. One of the four 1953 Coronation commemorative stamps, for example, was designed by Edmund Dulac. In 1958 regional definitives were introduced in response to the growing desire in Scotland, Wales and Northern Ireland for national and cultural identity.

By the 1960s designers were asking for the Wilding three-quarter view to be exchanged for a profile.

Wilding Definitives 1
The values ½d-2d were designed by
Enid Marx.

Wilding Definitives 2
Other designers used include
Farrar-Bell, Adshead, Dulac and Knipe.

Royal Assent
No stamps are printed without the
Queen's approval. Above a design by
Enid Marx that received assent.

High-Value Definitives
As distinct from thematic and
commemorative stamps, the term
definitive (such as those right) refers
to stamps that remain in issue year
after year.

Various initiatives began in 1961, but it was not until 1965 that the Postmaster General, Anthony Wedgwood Benn, was given permission by the Queen to commission a new portrait.

The new profile was created by the sculptor Andrew Machin, who made a succession of plaster casts which were photographed under a variety of lighting schemes. The Queen likes the Machin effigy very much because it is a durable, emblematic icon rather than a photographic likeness.

The first essays (trials) of the Machin definitives were produced in December 1966. Machin's classic design is in part based on the design of the 1840 Penny Black. The emblematic quality of Machin's portrait is an advantage to designers: the Queen's head can appear as a clear icon on any stamp, no matter how complicated the subject matter may be, without compromising or being compromised by the design.

Since the mid 1970s a silhouette version of the Machin cast has been used on the special issue stamps. It was Tony Benn who encouraged the Royal Mail to produce thematic stamps and the Royal Mail has since built up a considerable business with them. One most interesting series was 'Social Reformers', designed by David Gentleman in 1976. At the time they were considered dour: today they are collectors' items. The great variety of thematic stamps that has been produced since the mid 1960s makes the Royal Mail one of the most important patrons of contemporary artists and designers.

Machin's Icon
Right is the final cast approved by the Queen and far right is an early design. The Queen likes the Machin effigy for its emblematic, classical and enduring qualities.

The Machin Definitives
Left is a selection of the definitives derived from the Machin cast. The process, from start to finish, had taken over five years.

Such commemorative stamps as those for the Queen's coronation, the marriage of the Prince and Princess of Wales, the Queen's Silver Jubilee and the Queen Mother's ninetieth birthday have proved very successful with the public. They also provide an attractive 'family album' of the modern Royal Family.

The issue celebrating the fortieth anniversary of the Queen's reign has been designed by 'Why Not', a design consultancy run by graduates at the Royal College of Art. The informality and human interest of these latest stamps provide a visual summary of the way the relationship between the Sovereign and her subjects has progressed.

Thematic Stamps

Shown here is David Gentleman's 'Social Reformers' series and a selection of the very popular wildlife stamps.

Commemorative Stamps

These are normally used to mark a royal occasion. The current issue marks the 40th anniversary of the Queen's accession.

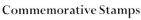

COINS AND BANKNOTES

THE CURRENCY OF THE UNITED KINGDOM emanates from two sources: the Royal Mint – which is responsible for coins – and the Bank of England – which produces the country's banknotes.

In the case of coins there have so far been two main series issued during the Queen's reign. The first, issued in 1953 following the Queen's accession to the throne, was in the same denominations as previously and was designed by Mary Gillick. With decimalization, the denominations naturally had to be changed and a new design by Arnold Machin, based on that used for stamps, was introduced. This has since been amended, with new designs by Raphael Maklouf, and the resulting coins were first issued in 1985.

In the case of banknotes there have also been two important series issued – the 'C' and the 'D' series. The 'C' series notes were the first to feature a portrait of the Queen, dropping the image of Britannia (designed by Daniel Maclise RA) which had appeared unaltered since 1855. The 'D' series is known as the Pictorial Series because it is the most highly illustrated in the history of British banknotes.

United Kingdom coins and banknotes are high quality designs rooted in craftsmanship but manufactured with speed, efficiency and security by advanced technology. But aside from aesthetics and economy, the other constant criterion shaping currency design is the need to defeat the forgers.

Shillings and Pence
Shown here are the reverse sides of the pre-decimal silver and bronze coins. The English and Scottish Shilling each had a different design.

New Pence
Once the Machin image had been chosen for obverse, the design interest focused on the reverse: over 1,000 designs were submitted for the various compositions.

The A Series

It is easy to see how the old white five pound note was big enough to wrap up the owl and the pussycat, not to mention their honey.

Commemorative Coins

Commemorative coins are rarely struck as the Queen is anxious not to devalue the significance of those which are issued. Shown here are the cast, the obverse and reverse sides of the Coronation Crown (top) and the Jubilee Crown (below).

The C Series

Produced in 1960, these were the first banknotes to feature an image of the Queen.

ROYAL MEMORABILIA

CERAMIC FIGURES AND DECORATED MUGS, plates and jugs, marking the coronation of monarchs and other royal occasions, have been produced by British potteries since the middle of the seventeenth century. Although design purists might raise their eyebrows at certain examples, the popularity of the genre with the public increases with every new event.

No official mugs were produced for the 1953 coronation, but this did not stop hundreds of thousands of mugs, cups, plates and tins from flooding the market. The prices they fetch today naturally vary according to the quality of the workmanship and, of course, their degree of rarity.

Some items of memorabilia have become both collectors' items and shrewd investments. For while it is true that run-of-the-mill mugs commemorating the coronations of Edward VII, George V and George VI are still cheap, those celebrating that of Queen Victoria can now fetch in excess of £1,000. Many mugs were also produced in anticipation of the coronation of Edward VIII, which of course did not happen, and now possess a certain curiosity value. Those actually marked 'Abdication' are much rarer and therefore more valuable.

Lidded Pot
This unusual pot is one of a limited edition of 200 made by Adderley China.

Loving Cup
It shows the royal coat of arms on the reverse side and was made by Paragon China of Stoke-on-Trent.

Tea-cup and saucer
Coronation bone china made by Rosina.

Trooping the Colour
This pottery loving cup (right) was commissioned by the brewers Courage & Co. from Royal Doulton.

Minton
A fine porcelain beaker.

Copeland Spode
An earthenware
beaker.

Royal Portrait
The photograph is by Dorothy Wilding.

Tea Caddy
Prince Philip appears on
the reverse side.

Pottery Mug
It shows the Marcus Adam portrait.

Teatime Trio
Royal Staffordshire produced
this bone-china cup,
saucer and plate in an
unlimited edition.

Lion and Unicorn
Two pint-sized mugs
by Wedgwood.

Tuscan Ware
A garland of
national emblems
frame the Queen.

Most of the memorabilia associated with Queen Elizabeth II have yet to become sought after as a serious investment, although there are believed to be thousands of people building complete collections of souvenirs associated with the Queen and her family. One of the rarest items is a commemorative Minton vase marking the marriage of Princess Elizabeth to Lieutenant Philip Mountbatten (HRH The Duke of Edinburgh). Although an edition of 500 vases was originally planned, it is believed that now only two survive.

The sort of commemorative memorabilia that intrigue collectors today are not those featuring the major occasions, but those which are more offbeat, such as the mug by the Staffordshire pottery Caverswall, that commemorated not the marriage but the betrothal of the Prince of Wales and Lady Diana Spencer.

Quality Street
A commemorative Silver Jubilee toffee tin, made by Mackintosh.

Caverswall China
A smiling portrait of the Queen surrounded by national emblems.

Walking Mug
An earthenware mug by Carlton.

Wedgwood
A pint-sized earthenware mug designed by Richard Guyatt.

Sutherland
A bone china mug, made for the Peter Jones collection, Wakefield.

Crown Staffordshire
Two pieces marking
the Silver Jubilee. The
plate (far right) is
from a limited edition
of 10,000.

Wedgwood
This ten-inch plate is
number 707 in a limited
edition of 1,000.

Queen and Consort
A decorative bone china
cup and saucer.

The ROYAL COLLECTION

THE ROYAL COLLECTION, held in trust for the nation by Queen Elizabeth II, is the largest private holding of works of art in the world. Bald statistics cannot fail to impress. For where the National Gallery in London has just over 2,000 paintings, the Royal Collection has about 7,000. In addition there are 30,000 drawings and watercolours, over 2,000 miniatures and about 500,000 prints.

Over the centuries royal collectors have displayed widely varying tastes. Among the most important collectors have been Henry VIII, Charles I, Frederick, Prince of Wales, George III, George IV, Queen Victoria and Prince Albert.

Sir Anthony Van Dyck
Van Dyck was for a time in the service of Charles I, perhaps the greatest and most ambitious British royal collector. This painting, 'The Five Eldest Children of Charles I' is one of his many famous portraits of the Royal Family.

Thomas Gainsborough
The paintings by Thomas Gainsborough in the
Royal Collection are unsurpassed. Shown here is
his portrait of 'Henry, Duke of Cumberland, with the
Duchess of Cumberland and Lady Elizabeth Lutterell'.

The Royal Collection has outstanding holdings of Dutch and English paintings, which include works by Rembrandt, Cuyp, Van Dyck, Reynolds and Gainsborough. The collection of Leonardo da Vinci and Holbein drawings is unparalleled, while the collections of Sèvres porcelain, French furniture, arms and armour are of the finest quality.

The Queen has made acquisitions of important historical portraits that relate to the British monarchy, its history and its institutions. Some acquisitions have been made to embellish specific houses. For Sandringham House the Queen bought 'Queen Alexandra with her three eldest grandchildren and her dogs' (1902) by Frederick Morgan and Thomas Blinks, and 'The Big Shoot' (1867) by Thomas Jones Barker.

In 1970 and again in 1989 the Queen acquired a series of elaborate drawings made by Morrel and Seddon dating from the early nineteenth century, which relate to George IV's extensive renovations of Windsor Castle. Other purchases include Blanchet's portraits of 'Bonnie Prince Charlie' and Prince Henry Benedict. A noteworthy acquisition in 1987 was Turner's topographical watercolour of Windsor Castle – to date the only work by Turner in the Collection.

The Royal Collection has also been enriched by appropriate gifts from both British subjects and from foreigners.

Bonnie Prince Charlie
Prince Charles Edward Stuart painted
by Blanchet (right).

Queen Victoria
A study from life of the young
Queen Victoria by Sir David Wilkie.

Edward VII
This painting of Edward VII when Prince of Wales on
Newmarket Heath, by Barraud, was acquired in 1990.

For example, 'Augustus, Duke of Sussex' (1803-4) by Domenico Pellegrini, was presented by the President of Portugal in 1978, while 'The Queen with her racehorse Aureole, her trainer Captain Cecil Boyd-Rochfort and jockey Eph Smith' (1957) by Sir Alfred Munnings, was given by Viscount Astor.

The Royal Collection is rich in animal paintings. In addition to a number of fine paintings by Stubbs, it has many by Landseer, whose work was a great favourite of Queen Victoria. The Queen has continued this tradition by commissioning several paintings of her favourite animals, including 'The Queen's nine Corgis and Dorgis' by Susan Crawford.

While the Collection was of course formed to furnish and adorn the royal palaces and residences, its treasures have often been placed on exhibition in the past, and during the Queen's stewardship more works of art have been made accessible to the public in this way than in any previous reign. In 1962 the Queen opened the Queen's Gallery at Buckingham Palace in which twenty-six major exhibitions of art drawn from the Collection have been held. In addition there is the Master Drawings Gallery at Windsor Castle, which opened in 1966.

Several important travelling exhibitions have been organized and among the most imaginative was the Queen's 1977 Jubilee exhibition in Australia. The paintings and other works of art were mounted on a train and taken all over Australia by rail.

George Stubbs
The British passion for animals is
reflected in the popularity of animal
painters. This painting (below) by
Stubbs is of 'Laetitia, Lady Lade'.

Sir Edwin Landseer
Landseer is here represented by
his painting (right) of Queen
Victoria's favourite pets, 'Hector,
Nero and Dash with the Parrot, Lory'.

CONSERVATION AND SCHOLARSHIP

D URING THE PRESENT REIGN emphasis has been placed on conservation, and the Collection has benefited from a high degree of expertise and scholarship. Specialized workshops have been set up to treat the paintings, pictures and other works of art in the Collection. In 1953 a furniture restoration workshop was established at Marlborough House, followed by a studio for the conservation of works on paper at Windsor Castle in 1971, an armoury at Marlborough House in 1974 and a paintings conservation studio at St James Palace in 1981.

One of the most impressive conservation projects undertaken by the Royal Collection was the cleaning and restoration of eight of the nine paintings, 'The Triumphs of Caesar' by Andrea Mantegna. This work, which spanned twelve years, was carried out at Hampton Court by John Brealey, assisted by Joan Seddon.

Conservation
John Brealey at work
on 'The Triumphs of Caesar'.

The exhibitions in The Queen's Gallery have provided the opportunity to examine and treat many of the paintings and, with advances in conservation techniques, discoveries have been made, leading in some cases to changes in attribution. For example, the painting by Pieter Bruegel the Elder now entitled 'Massacre of the Innocents' was, prior to its restoration, thought to be of the school of Bruegel and its true subject was not known. Another recent discovery was made by Dr Martin Postle of an unfinished portrait of Shakespeare under Gainsborough's painting of Johann Christian Fischer. His suspicions of the existence of the portrait were confirmed by X-radiography.

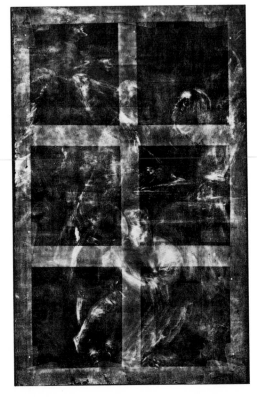

Massacre of the Innocents

This is just one of a number of paintings Pieter Bruegel the Elder and his school made of this scene from the 1560s onwards. By 1660 it had undergone a remarkable transformation when almost all the references to the Biblical story of the 'Massacre of the Innocents' were suppressed and the painting was consequently described as 'The Sacking of a Village'. A cleaning in 1987 revealed traces of Bruegel's signature and the high quality of the brushwork and handling of detail, while infra-red reflectography disclosed the presence of the original massacred infants hidden by seventeenth century overpaint.

Shakespeare Revealed

When Thomas Gainsborough's portrait of Johann Christian Fischer was X-rayed in 1991, it was discovered that another painting lay underneath. Through the researches of Dr Martin Postle, since confirmed by scientific analysis, it has been established that Gainsborough painted over his own portrait of Shakespeare.

The CASSON SUITE

WHEN SIR HUGH CASSON was commissioned to redesign a suite of the Queen's private rooms at Windsor Castle, a committee of distinguished art experts was set up to assemble a collection of modern paintings from which the Queen and the Duke of Edinburgh could make a selection to decorate the Casson suite.

Casson's interior designs, done in 1960, incorporate the plain angularity of the period – it was a time when plain, undecorated Scandinavian design was fashionable and ornament was generally regarded as superfluous by both designers and architects.

However, the eleven works chosen by the Queen and Prince Philip contribute an exciting infusion of colour, gesture and visual interest to the suite. The chosen works include paintings by Alan Davie, Roger de Grey, Sir William Dobell, Barbara Hepworth, Ivon Hitchens, Sir Sidney Nolan and Graham Sutherland. The selection is interesting not only for its quality, but for its diversity, ranging from the sympathetic naturalism of some works to the extravagant abstraction of others. The choice demonstrates that the Queen and the Duke of Edinburgh's interests extend beyond naturalistic art.

The Casson Suite
One of the rooms designed by Sir Hugh Casson.

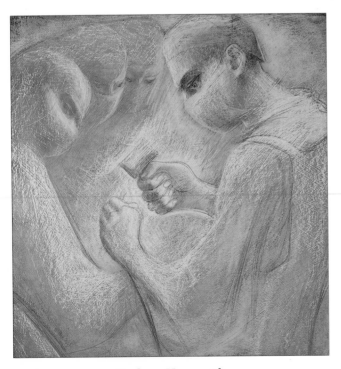

Barbara Hepworth
Her painting, 'Arthrodesis of the Hip', (above) was one of the studies she made in the 1950s of the National Health Service at work.

Alan Davie
'Throne of the Eye Goddess' (right) is one of the few non-representational works acquired by the Queen.

Sir Sidney Nolan
Sir Sidney, one of Australia's most eminent painters, is a particular favourite of the Duke of Edinburgh. This painting is entitled 'Australian Landscape' (opposite right).

Graham Sutherland
Graham Sutherland became nationally famous for his design 'Christ in Majesty', the great tapestry commissioned for Sir Basil Spence's rebuilt Coventry Cathedral. This painting is called 'The Armillary Sphere' (below).

ROYAL COLLECTORS

HENRY VIII, who was the first monarch to start assembling a collection of works of art, could be described as the founder of the Royal Collection. Among the most attractive sculptures surviving from his collection is a painted terracotta bust of a boy, believed to be of Henry himself as a child. Today the collection of sculpture amounts to approximately 1,400 pieces, many of the most important having been acquired by George IV.

The collection of decorative and applied art grew substantially in the eighteenth and nineteenth centuries. George III and George IV, especially the latter, were major collectors in almost every field of applied art, with clocks being a particular interest. George III commissioned several astronomical clocks – a natural adjunct to his passion for science and astronomy – and he also commissioned timepieces from many of the leading English horologists. George IV built up a collection of French clocks, which included an outlandish digital clock by Jean-Antoine Lepine in the form of a bust of a negress in whose eyes the time is displayed, the minutes in one, the hours in the other.

It was also George IV who formed the unrivalled collection of eighteenth-century Sèvres porcelain.

Bust of Henry VIII
Dated *circa* 1500 and attributed to Guido Mazzoni, this rare early coloured terracotta bust of Henry VIII is one of the prizes of the extensive royal sculpture collection.

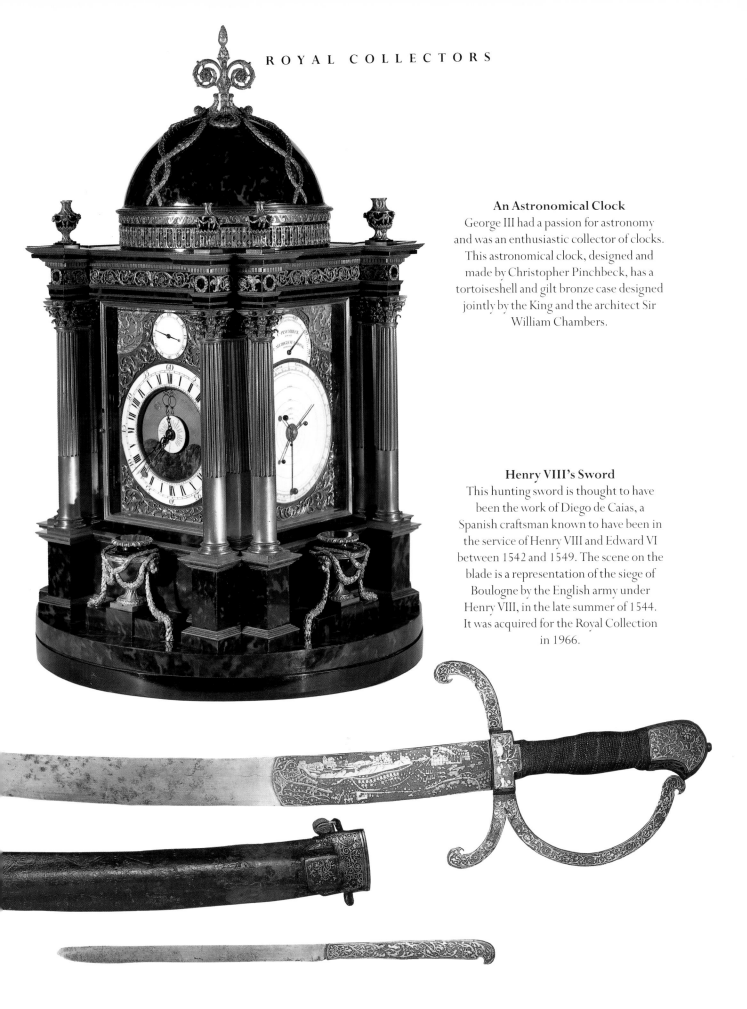

An Astronomical Clock

George III had a passion for astronomy and was an enthusiastic collector of clocks. This astronomical clock, designed and made by Christopher Pinchbeck, has a tortoiseshell and gilt bronze case designed jointly by the King and the architect Sir William Chambers.

Henry VIII's Sword

This hunting sword is thought to have been the work of Diego de Caias, a Spanish craftsman known to have been in the service of Henry VIII and Edward VI between 1542 and 1549. The scene on the blade is a representation of the siege of Boulogne by the English army under Henry VIII, in the late summer of 1544. It was acquired for the Royal Collection in 1966.

It includes a number of dinner services of which the most lavish is one commissioned by Louis XVI for his own personal use at Versailles. Begun in 1783, it was left incomplete following the King's execution in 1793. In addition the Collection possesses about 170 ornamental vases.

George IV also bought substantial quantities of silver gilt. Many of his commissions, placed with Rundell, Bridge and Rundell, were for the Grand Service which was intended for use only at Carlton House.

George IV's interests covered a wide range of decorative arts and another notable collection was of European and Oriental arms and armour, both ancient and modern.

His father, George III, commissioned some fine examples of cabinet-making from William Vile, who was appointed cabinet-maker to the King in 1761. Recognized as one of the most accomplished craftsmen of his time he supplied the King and Queen Charlotte with pieces notable 'for superb finish...originality of design, with carving of the highest quality'. But no monarch matched the spending of George IV, who bought furniture, both

Rococo Centrepiece
Paul Crespin, the English Huguenot silversmith, made this rococo silver-gilt centrepiece for Frederick Prince of Wales in 1741-2.

Sèvres Vase
George IV built up a substantial collection of wares from this famous French factory between 1783 and 1829.

English and French, for Windsor Castle and Buckingham Palace, and commissioned pieces in the Chinese style for the Royal Pavilion in Brighton. Among his most outstanding purchases is a jewel cabinet by Jean-Henri Riesener, which had been commissioned *circa* 1780 by the Comtesse de Provence, the wife of the future Louis XVIII. George IV, who particularly favoured furniture in the Louis XVI style, largely furnished his London residence, Carlton House (demolished in 1827), with French pieces.

The furniture and furnishing schemes commissioned by George IV for Windsor were for the most part designed by Englishmen and made by English cabinet-makers, although there are some major pieces of French applied art, such as the fine Gobelins tapestries which hang in the Queen's Presence and Audience Chambers. Later in the nineteenth century Prince Albert chose many of the furnishings for the two new royal residences he designed – Osborne House and Balmoral Castle. The furniture includes some unusual pieces, such as the German 'antler' furniture in the Horn Room at Osborne House.

The Queen has continued the tradition of acquiring decorative objects, especially pieces which are linked historically with her forebears.

Jewel Cabinet
William Vile was an outstanding cabinet-maker. This piece was made for George III.

The FABERGÉ COLLECTION

PETER CARL FABERGÉ (1846-1920) was a Russian goldsmith and jeweller. His father Gustav had opened a jewellery shop in St Petersburg in 1842 and Peter, having travelled extensively in Europe, took over the family firm in 1870. With his younger brother Agathon he built a company employing five hundred designers, goldsmiths, modellers, enamellers and gem cutters, until its disbandment in 1918.

The most famous Fabergé curios are the extravagant and elaborate Easter eggs. Each egg, whose shell is encrusted with precious and semi-precious gems, opens to reveal a surprise inside – a carved stone flower, a little statue or an enamelled portrait. The workshops also made cigarette cases, picture frames, and sprays of flowers made from jewels and gold, standing in rock-crystal vases.

The collection of Fabergé owned by the Queen is one of the most important in the world. Most of the pieces were inherited from King Edward VII and Queen Alexandria, while George VI collected Fabergé cigarette cases.

The Mosaic Egg
An Easter present for Tsarina Alexandra Feodorovna from Tsar Nicholas II in 1914, it was bought by George V and Queen Mary in 1934. This yellow gold and platinum egg contains a surprise in the form of an oval medallion with a painting of the Russian Royal children.

Caesar
A model in chalcedony of Edward VII's border terrier. Caesar's collar is inscribed 'I belong to the King'.

Kangaroo
One of a whole series of exotic animals that Fabergé created, it is made out of spinach jade.

Penguin
The main body is of
variegated grey chalcedony
and it has rose diamond eyes
and red gold feet.

The Egg Clock
Originally bought by Tsar
Nicholas II for his wife, it
came later into the collection
of Queen Mary. The clock
commemorates the birth of
Tsarevitch Nicholas in 1904
and is conceived as a Temple
of Love. The Tsarevitch is
symbolized by the cupid on
top of the egg and his four
sisters by the four cherubs at
the base.

Litter of Piglets
These four sleeping piglets were
crafted from different kinds
of chalcedony.

Hippopotamus
Fabergé created a number of
hippopotamuses; this one is
carved from obsidian, a glassy
volcanic rock.

*W*INDSOR

WINDSOR CASTLE is a romantic collection of large buildings set in five thousand acres of park and farm land. The thousand-room royal residence began as a wooden fort in the 1070s, built for William the Conqueror and a century later it was rebuilt in stone. The royal appartments were extended in the 1360s by Edward III, founder of the Order of the Garter, who built St George's Hall for the Knights of the Garter.

In 1475 foundations were laid for one of Britain's finest late-medieval buildings – St George's Chapel. This exceptional example of Perpendicular Gothic, completed by Henry VIII, contains the tombs of ten former sovereigns, including the late King George VI.

Charles II made considerable alterations to the State Apartments and commissioned work by several eminent craftsmen including Britain's finest carver, Grinling Gibbons. He also laid out the gracious three-mile Long Walk which runs south from the castle into Windsor Great Park.

Riding at Windsor

By foot or from horseback the view from the Long Walk towards the Castle is imposing. It is every tourist's idea of how a castle should be. This is no accident because in some respects the Castle has been styled into a modern conception of what a picturesque old castle should look like. This restyling occurred in the 1820s when King George

Turner's Windsor
Turner's painting, 'Windsor Castle from the Great Park', was acquired by the Queen in 1987. It is the first Turner to belong to the Royal Collection.

Waterloo Chamber
In this room hangs
the famous series of
Sir Thomas Lawrence
portraits of all those who
played a prominent part
in the defeat of Napoleon.

Fabergé's Windsor
This bonbonnière is
one of a pair, the other
depicting Balmoral.

IV commissioned the architect Sir Jeffry Wyatville to remodel the buildings with Gothic crenellations, towers and turrets. An open courtyard was covered over to form the Waterloo Chamber (in commemoration of the defeat of Napoleon at the battle of Waterloo), which is now used to host receptions and other formal occasions. The old fourteenth-century St George's Hall, the largest room in the Castle, was also altered and extended at this time. Today it is used by the Queen for state banquets.

Like her predecessors the Queen has made some changes. In the 1960s she commissioned Sir Hugh Casson to refurbish some of her private rooms and to redesign and redecorate the Royal Family's Private Chapel.

Today Windsor is in frequent use by the Queen, who spends her weekends there, as well as Easter and Royal Ascot week. Her private apartments have been described as 'country house with an emphasis upon comfort rather than opulence'. The public has access to the State Apartments, St George's Chapel and several other parts of the Castle and its grounds.

SANDRINGHAM

SANDRINGHAM, in the north of Norfolk, is perhaps the least regal-looking of the large royal houses and this is a part of its charm. Built in the late eighteenth century and acquired for the Prince of Wales in 1862, it was rebuilt as a Jacobean shooting lodge to house hundreds of people. To this day it retains an Edwardian atmosphere. This rambling country house was a great favourite of the Queen's father, George VI, who was born in Sandringham – and died there in 1952.

The house was larger in George VI's day. The Queen has had ninety of the four hundred rooms demolished because the house was becoming uneconomic. Indeed Sandringham is a good example of the Queen's general policy

Victorian Sandringham

The Prince of Wales and party in 'A Big Shoot at Sandringham in 1867' by Thomas Jones Barker (below). York Cottage (right), in the grounds of Sandringham.

The Small Drawing Room
The portrait above the bookcase
is of Queen Louise of Denmark
It was painted by
August Schiatt.

to make what she has inherited streamlined and efficient. She has not commissioned new houses for herself. The estate, however, has grown: originally 7,000 acres, it now covers 20,000 acres, half leased out to tenant farmers. There are extensive orchards, woodlands and a country park which is open to the public.

The estate is skilfully managed for conservation and profit: it grows and fells softwood timber on a renewable basis. Sandringham has its own sawmill and produces a wide range of timber products such as sheds and fences. In 1979-80 new glasshouses were built and these have automated equipment to regulate heating, irrigation and ventilation.

As a child the Queen spent her first Christmas at Sandringham and now, as Queen, she stays at Sandringham for Christmas and the New Year. It is a family home and it houses a number of the pictures collected by the Queen and the Duke of Edinburgh for their personal pleasure. Sandringham is also home to the royal labradors and spaniels which are bred as gun dogs for use by the Royal Family and keepers on the royal estates. The Queen takes a keen interest in the success of the kennels, which have prospered during her reign, and all the dogs are named by the Queen herself and registered at the Kennel Club with the prefix Sandringham.

Fabergé's Sandringham
A nephrite frame surrounds a view of Sandringham.
The duckling (right) is in cream quartzite.

The QUEEN'S HORSES

HORSE-RACING AND HORSE-BREEDING are two of the Queen's passions and they are both areas where her expertise is considerable. She is an expert judge of a horse, has an extensive knowledge of pedigrees and is respected as a sound reader of the form. Her particular interest is flat-racing and her horses have won four of the five English Classics – the Derby has so far eluded her.

The Queen owned her first pony in 1931 and as a child rode ponies over the moors at Balmoral; but it was at Windsor during the Second World War that she became proficient at horse care and stable management.

The first major race won by a royal horse that the Queen saw was when Hypericum won the 1000 Guineas in 1946. She inherited the Royal Studs on the death of her father in 1952 and had to wait only two years before Aureole won the Hardwicke

Aureole
Munnings captures the Queen with Aureole. Bred by George VI, Aureole gained his brilliant victories in the colours of the Queen. These included the King George VI and Queen Elizabeth Diamond Stakes in 1954.

The Queen at Ascot
Like every owner, the Queen is happiest when her horses come in first.

Stakes at Royal Ascot, following it in the same year with the King George VI and Queen Elizabeth Diamond Stakes. Another great royal racing success from the 1950s was Almeria. In the Queen's Silver Jubilee year of 1977 the star of her stables was Dunfermline who, with a developed sense of history, won The Oaks and the St Leger.

Today the Royal Studs are divided between Sandringham and Wolferton in Norfolk and Polhampton in Berkshire. The stallions, mares and foals are based at Sandringham, while the yearlings are kept at Polhampton, the stud the Queen bought in 1972. Each year, the Queen has about twenty-five horses in training with the Earl of Huntingdon and Ian Balding.

The Queen's racing manager is the Earl of Carnarvon and although the Queen's passion for horses is one of her major pastimes, it is run as a business (although privately financed). The intention is to win races and breed good horses and many of the successes enjoyed by the Queen and her managers have been in races run in Europe and the USA.

On Horseback
The Queen is herself an accomplished equestrian. As a child she rode ponies over the moors at Balmoral.

Sandringham Stud
Sandringham (left) is home to one of the three royal studs, the others being at Wolferton in Norfolk and Polhampton in Berkshire.

The QUEEN'S DOGS

THE QUEEN IS FAMOUS for her fondness for corgis, less so for her liking of labradors. The eleven corgis were as outraged as anyone else when, on 9 July 1982, the Queen found an intruder, Michael Fagan, in her bedroom. According to Elizabeth Longford, whilst a footman and a maid manoeuvred Fagan into a pantry, the Queen kept off 'the indignant corgis' who had arrived with the footman like a canine cavalry regiment.

There has been a corgi in the Royal Family since 1933 and the Queen received the first of her own corgis, called Susan, in 1944. Her corgis today are Susan's descendants. There is also a breed of dog special to the Queen – the royal

Nine Corgis and Dorgis
Like her great-great-grandmother Queen Victoria, the
Queen commissions paintings of her favourite animals.
Sue Crawford painted this Sandringham group in 1980.

The Queen with her Labradors
The photograph was taken
by Elizabeth Johnston
at Sandringham in 1977.

'dorgi'; this is the consequence of a corgi mating with Princess Margaret's dachshund.

The dogs are part of the family and they travel with the Queen on internal flights with the Queen's Flight or on the Royal Train. The Queen keeps her labradors at Sandringham and four field trial champions have been trained here. Indeed it is the policy of the Sandringham kennels to train to high field trial standards as many of the dogs as are suitable.

Today there are approximately twenty dogs at the kennels, the more experienced of whom act as gundogs for the Royal Family during the shooting season, while the younger ones are still under training.

Susan's Grave
The Queen was given her
first corgi, Susan,
on her eighteenth birthday.

At Home
The Queen and Queen
Elizabeth the Queen Mother
surrounded by friends
at Sandringham (above).

ℛOYAL PATRONAGE

IN THE LAST FORTY YEARS the business of charity has become just that: business. The big charities are powerful organizations that may occasionally be controversial because they are professional pressure groups, often critical of our own and foreign governments' policies. Consequently none of the Royal Family, the Queen especially, becomes a patron lightly. To have the Queen as a patron of your voluntary body or charity confers both status and respectability. The Queen does accept temporary as well as permanent appointments as a patron but will sometimes seek ministerial advice and will, in any case, patronize only those bodies that have a proven record of usefulness, competence and integrity.

Unsurprisingly the Queen's name is associated with hundreds of voluntary bodies, partly because she took over so many patronages from George VI at the time of her accession. Yet even with these ex-officio appointments, the Queen likes to be seen as more than just a figurehead and has sought to attend an event of each of the nearly 800 charities to which her name is attached. The same is true of Queen Elizabeth the Queen Mother, coming as she does from an age when patronage was more lightly bestowed.

Covent Garden
The Queen greeting members of
the congregation at a Thanksgiving
Service in 1988.

Some charitable events, especially the Royal Maundy, have ancient beginnings and have become a part of the nation's fabric of symbolism and unity. Each year, on the thursday before Good Friday, the Queen distributes the Maundy Money, silver coins minted for the occasion. The recipients are Christian pensioners who have been nominated by their clergy to receive the money in recognition of their service to the Church and the community. The recipients are chosen from all Christian denominations and the Queen initiated the policy of having the Maundy service in a different cathedral each year. The roots of the Maundy practice go back as far as AD 600.

Other royal charity connections are much younger, such as those with the Women's Institute. The National Federation of Women's Institutes (NFWI) is one of only a few voluntary bodies to have more than one member of the Royal Family as a patron – both the Queen and Queen Elizabeth the Queen Mother are members of the Sandringham branch of the WI. They are also both patrons of Britain's largest children's charity, Barnardo's, which also has a third royal, the Princess of Wales, as its President.

Children's charities are a significant part of the royal patronage list. The Princess Royal, Princess Anne, has been intensely involved with the organization and the public profile of the Save the Children Fund and has to a great extent led from the front. The Duke of Edinburgh takes his responsibilities as a patron very seriously and he is perhaps best known for being the International President of the Worldwide Fund for Nature (WWF). He is a strong, forthright speaker and an important propagandist for conservation and wildlife. It is important to note that these senior positions demand involvement and not simply being 'a name'. Recently, with the spread of the new disease AIDS, the Princess of Wales has attracted praise and respect for her public support of AIDS victims, especially at a time when some people responded to sufferers, some of whom are children, by shunning them. The Prince of Wales has taken the cause of young people, especially in the inner cities, very much to his heart and like each senior member of the Royal family has approached his patronage work with a thoroughness that goes far beyond merely being 'a name'.

Albert Hall
The Queen, Patron of the Save the Children Fund, and the Princess Royal, President, at the Joy to the World Concert, December 1989.

A CONTINUING PURPOSE

THE VISIBLE WORK OF THE QUEEN includes ceremonial occasions, banquets, state visits, tours of factories and the opening of new buildings. Even the bestowing of honours is quite a public event with friends and relatives of the newly honoured watching as the Queen bestows the medals and decorations of honour. She often manages to see 130 or more people in little over an hour – and each award is accompanied by a smile and some special words for the recipient.

But the hidden work of the Queen is as important as her ceremonial and public duties. Much of her work is directed towards keeping herself well-informed on parliamentary, ministerial, national and international affairs. Without such knowledge the Queen could not properly fulfil her duties as Head of State, and the rights that she has as a constitutional monarch – to be consulted, to encourage and to warn – would be hollow.

Wherever the Queen happens to be – at home or abroad – there is a constant stream of letters and Foreign Office and Cabinet Office papers. Her Press

Secretary provides daily summaries of royal coverage in the newspapers and when Parliament is sitting, the Vice-Chamberlain of the Household provides a daily report of its proceedings. The Foreign Office conveys information to the Queen about international affairs whilst those Commonwealth countries of which the Queen is Head of State have access to the Queen's offices – they are not filtered through a British government department.

The Commonwealth Mace and Goblets

Commissioned by the Royal Anniversary Trust, the Commonwealth mace (below) is a gift to the Queen, marking the fortieth anniversary of her accession to the throne. The gold mace, designed by Gerald Benney, Goldsmith and Silversmith to the Queen, from an idea of Robin Gill, is surmounted by the Royal Coat of Arms and a cabochon ruby. The stem is a gold spiral which incorporates the fifty Commonwealth flags, painted on enamel. To accompany the mace are fifty gold-plated toasting goblets, given by and bearing the symbols of each nation of the Commonwealth.

All foreign ambassadors present their credentials to the Queen when appointed; all formally take their leave of her when their period of duty is ended. All British ambassadors and High Commissioners are received by the Queen as they are formally Her Majesty's representatives abroad.

As everyone in a position to know will assert, the Queen is now the most experienced statesman in the world. In her Christmas message broadcast on 25 December 1991 she said, 'I feel the same obligation to you that I felt in 1952. With your prayers, and your help, and with the love and support of my family, I shall try to serve you in the years to come.' The work goes on.

The Queen in 1991
This photograph by David Secombe, Sir Harry Secombe's son,
was given to the Royal Anniversary Trust by Buckingham Palace.

PLAN OF THE EXHIBITION

The Queen as World Leader
A State Banquet
Anatomy of a Royal Tour

Queen and Commonwealth
Commonwealth Map
Commonwealth Visits
Commonwealth Gifts

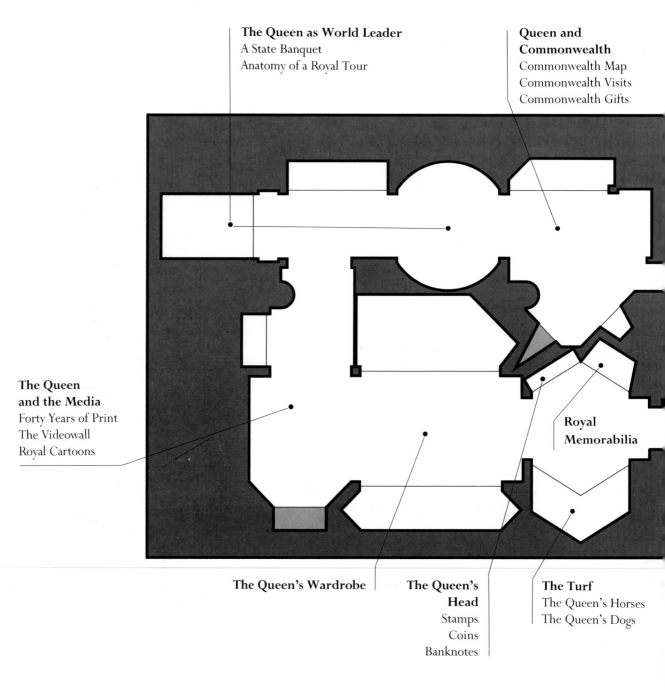

The Queen and the Media
Forty Years of Print
The Videowall
Royal Cartoons

Royal Memorabilia

The Queen's Wardrobe

The Queen's Head
Stamps
Coins
Banknotes

The Turf
The Queen's Horses
The Queen's Dogs

The Royal Collection
Paintings and Drawings
New Acquisitions
Conservation and Scholarship
Decorative Arts
Fabergé

PLAN OF THE EXHIBITION

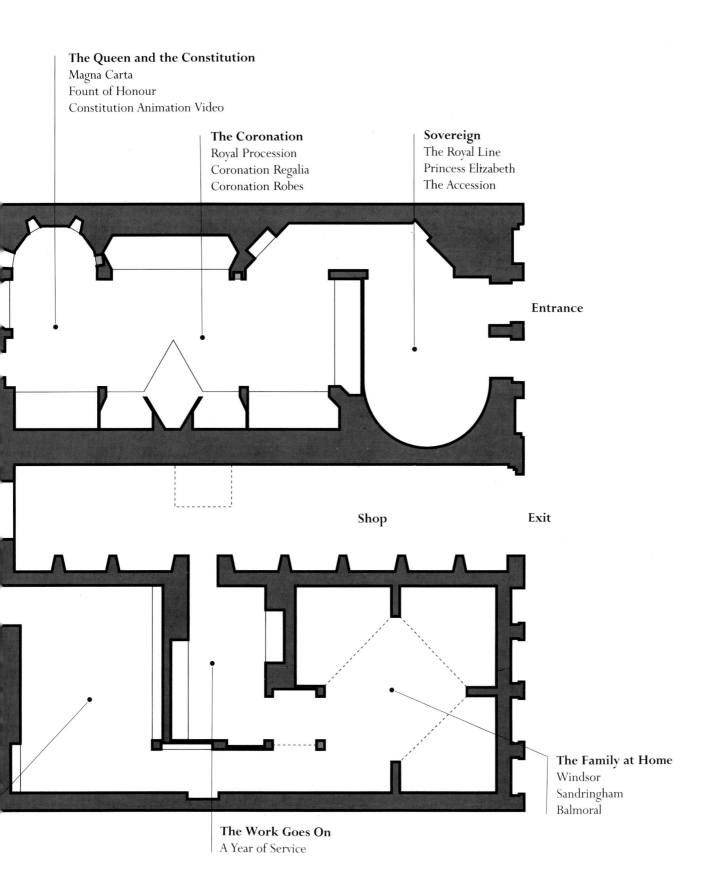

The Queen and the Constitution
Magna Carta
Fount of Honour
Constitution Animation Video

The Coronation
Royal Procession
Coronation Regalia
Coronation Robes

Sovereign
The Royal Line
Princess Elizabeth
The Accession

Entrance

Shop

Exit

The Family at Home
Windsor
Sandringham
Balmoral

The Work Goes On
A Year of Service

$\mathscr{A}$CKNOWLEDGEMENTS

Exhibition Acknowledgements

Sovereign Executive Committee
Jocelyn Stevens (Chairman), John Julius Norwich (Curator), Professor Christopher Frayling (College Curator), Ruth Anders (Project Director), Gerald Margolis (Finance Director), Professor Theo Crosby, Pedro Guedes, John Thackara, Hilary Bracegirdle, Julia Hawkins.

Special thanks to BBC Television, British Pathe News and Independent Television News. Additional archive footage supplied by British Movietone News and Central Office of Information.

Design by Pentagram. Research and procurement by Design Analysis International. Videowall by IE. Archive film research by Illuminations. Exhibition contractors – Button Eventures.

Picture Acknowledgements

Reproduced by gracious permission of Her Majesty the Queen: 14 above, 42, 43, 45, 46, 47, 48, 49, below, 97 middle. Royal Collection, St James's Palace © 1992 Her Majesty the Queen: 21 below, 30 above, 31 left, 36 above, 44, 74, 75, 76, 77, 78, 79, 80, 81, 82, 83 above, 84, 85, 86, 87, 89, 91, 93 below, 94 below. Windsor Castle, Royal Library © 1992 Her Majesty the Queen: 90 below. Reproduced by kind permission of His Royal Highness the Duke of Edinburgh © reserved: 59 below, 62, 63, 83 below.

Specially commissioned photography by Geoff Dann: 14, 15, 31 right, 33, 42, 43, 45, 46, 47, 48, 49, 52, 53, 54 below, 55, 57, 64, 65, 66, 67, 70, 71, 72, 73.

Bodleian Library, Oxford: 35. The British Architectural Library: 28, 29 above left. Camera Press: front cover, 8, 16 (1931, 1935, 1938), 17 (1941, 1942, 1944, 1945, 1948), 23. The College of Arms: 14 below. The Estate Office, Sandringham: 92, 93 above, 95 above. The Governor and Company of the Bank of England: 69 above and right. Tim Graham: 40, 51 below, 94 above. Glenn Harvey: 95 below. Hulton Picture Company: 17 (1951), 18 below, 29 below and right column. Anwar Hussein: 41, 49 above, 50, 51 above, 97 below. Mirror Pictures: 17 (1950). Museum of London: 20-21 (coach). The National Postal Museum: back cover, 2, 64, 65, 66, 67. Neils Obee: 56. Popperfoto: 16 (1926, 1927, 1928, 1929, 1930, 1932, 1934, 1936), 17 (1939, 1940, 1946, 1947), 18 above left, 21 above. Press Association: 16 (1933, 1937). Reproduced by courtesy of Sir Hardy Amies: 52, 53. Reproduced by courtesy of Susan Crawford: 96. Reproduced by courtesy of the Dean and Chapter of Westminster: 27 above left, middle left and below left. Reproduced by courtesy of Morris Green: 30 below, 54. Reproduced by courtesy of Hope and Glory: 70, 71, 72, 73. Reproduced by courtesy of Elizabeth Johnston: 97 above. Reproduced by courtesy of Simone Mirman: 57. Reproduced by courtesy of Captain George Mitcherson: 31 right, 54 right, 55. Reproduced by courtesy of Mr Stewart Blacker: 15. Reproduced by courtesy of Hugo Vickers: 19 right, 22. Reproduced by courtesy of the Worshipful Company of Glovers of London and the Museum of Costume, Bath: 27 right. Reproduced by permission of the Controller of Her Majesty's Stationery Office: 24, 25, 26. © The Royal Anniversary Trust: 100, 101. The Royal Mint: 68, 69 middle and below left. Save the Children Fund – Doug Mackenzie : 99. Spink and son: 36 below left and right, 37. Syndication International: 17 (1943, 1949). Topham Pictures: 19.